The Yellow Caravan

NORFOLK DOCUMENTS

Norfolk is fortunate in having a wealth of documents surviving from the past millennium. Many are cared for in the Norfolk Record Office at the Archive Centre in Norwich; others remain in private collections. Some documents (and audiovisual materials) are now available online; a few have been published in scholarly editions. However, there remain many fascinating papers known only to specialist researchers or held with family members. The intent of this NORFOLK DOCUMENTS series is to bring some of these to a wider readership, taking advantage of recent short-run printing technology to present them at reasonable cost for anyone with an interest in East Anglian history.

Instead of being restricted to reproducing what the original author wrote, with all its puzzles of historical reference and sometime quirky handwriting, this series includes:

careful transcriptions of the documents;
introductions to set the originals in their historical context;
notes to clarify obscure allusions;
references to further reading;
pictures, either from the original documents or from other sources;
indexing of people, places, themes.

Also in the *Norfolk Documents* Series:

1. Mr Marten's Travels in East Anglia   *Elizabeth Larby*
2. A History of Swaffham National Schools *David Butters with Olive Wilson*
3. I Therefore Post Him as a Coward   *Gill Blanchard*

Pages specially compiled to support this book are available on the Poppyland website. These can be found at:

https://poppyland.co.uk/index.php?ref=CARAVANACTS

The Yellow Caravan

Camping Round Norfolk in 1912

The 1912 Norfolk ballad (and diary) of Honor Elwes

Juliet Webster

POPPYLAND PUBLISHING

This edition 2019 published by Poppyland Publishing, Lowestoft, NR32 3BB.

www.poppyland.co.uk

ISBN 978 1 909796 67 6

Designed and typeset in 10.5 on 13.5 pt Gilamesh Pro.

Printed by Ashford Colour Press.

Picture credits:
Author, cover, 19 (top), 21, 23, 24, 34, 42, 74, 86, 90, 98.
Author's collection 11, 12, 13, 14, 15, 16, 18, 26, 29, 32 (top), 47, 50, 53, 54, 60, 61, 63, 66, 68, 72 (bottom), 73, 76, 82, 83 (left), 84, 88 (bottom), 91, 92 (top), 93, 96, 97, 102 (top), 106, 109, 112, 115, 120 (middle), 124, 126, 132.
Brown, E. 37 (bottom).
Button, M. 40*, 62*.
David, 32 (bottom)*.
Dixon, D. 123*.
Elwes, B. back cover (inset) 20, 27, 28, 30, 31, 36, 37 (top), 38 (bottom), 41, 43, 45 (bottom), 46, 48, 56, 57, 58, 59, 64 (top), 69, 70 (bottom), 72 (top), 77, 80 (bottom), 81, 83 (right), 85, 88 (top), 94, 95, 100, 101, 102 (bottom), 103, 104, 105, 107, 108, 111, 116, 117, 118, 120 (bottom), 121.
Fielding, J. 114*.
Guffogg, J.P. 70 (top)*.
Hurford, P. 51*.
Lubbock family, 120 (top).
Peter Brooks collection, 55, 64 (bottom), 65.
Picture Norfolk, 71, 45 (top), 92 (bottom).
Poppyland collection, 38 (top), 80 (top).
Poringland History Group, 110.
Trenowath family 17, 19 (bottom).

* reproduced under Creative Commons Licence.

Acknowledgements

The author would like to thank the following for their help and support in the preparation and writing of this book:

Ben Elwes and the Elwes family, Giles Currie, John Thornton, Ronnie & Shirley Gedge, the Bullard family, the Cubitt family, Jeremy Greenwood, John Pockett, Nigel Savory, Jean Joice, Charlotte Crawley, Mary Athill, the Don family, the McCarthy family, the Lubbock family, the Gurney family, Richard Blake, April Falcon, Tricia Blakesley and the Trenowath family, Bill Lewis, Sir Michael Savory & the Muckleburgh Collection, Peter Walsingham of Wells, Simon Knott, Sir Richard Jewson, Scilla Landale, the late Jennifer Shaw, Jane Macfarlane, Nicolette Hallett, Mr & Mrs Hipperson, Diana Cooke, Mark Dugdale, Brian Wright. R G Carter Group, Voluntary Force Historian Norfolk Constabulary, Norfolk Wildlife Trust, The Broads Authority, National Trust, Gresham's School Archive, Norfolk Record Office, Norwich Writers' Circle, Poringland Archive Group, The Roman Catholic Diocese of East Anglia, Thimbleby & Shorland, Norwich Castle Museum, Norfolk Heritage Centre, The Forum Library, Norfolk County Council, Visit Norfolk, Holkham Archive, Blakeney History Society, Norfolk Horse-Driving Club, Eastern Daily Press, Thursford Collection.

Contents

Foreword

Apart from the enterprise of the original travellers you have done a remarkable job in getting the story into a form where we, a hundred years later, can enjoy it.

For me it is so interesting to get that insight into my mother in the years before she married and of course before my brother and I were on the scene. I so wish that we could throw some sort of switch to know our parents as they then were. Much younger of course than we are now! When they have become parents we as children only know them in that way and however dear to us, as my parents were to me, the relationship is different. I should have loved to see my mother and the others being cheeky to the policeman etc.

John Thornton, Harleston, Norfolk

Son of the Rev. & Mrs Jack Thornton formerly Miss Judith Birkbeck.

Preface

None of this would have been possible without the generosity of my cousin Jim Le Coq. He inherited from his aunt Honora (Honor) Elwes several boxes of paper, manuscripts and diaries which he passed to me in the 1970s to do whatever I liked with. Jim knew I enjoyed sorting paper—a pastime I had inherited from my paternal grandmother. In one of my many house moves, I opened a box to remind myself what was in it, and at the top lay the manuscript of Aunt Honor's lengthy poem in her extremely legible handwriting. I recognised exactly what it was, because I had previously found photographs of that same trip as well as Honor's leather-bound diary relating to it. Once I had made my move, I set about combining all three to make a story.

I copied the sepia photographs which had been taken with Box Brownie cameras. All three young ladies are likely to have owned these simple cameras since their teenage years: the Box Brownie having first become popular in 1900. At Holkham in May 2012 to mark the 100 years of the original journey I recited the poem and showed the pictures. When I moved into Norwich and joined the Norwich Writers Circle, I entered *The Yellow Caravan* into a short essay competition on a historic event which had taken place in Norfolk. Not only did I win the Past Search Trophy for Non-Fiction but Gareth Davies of Poppyland had generously guaranteed the winning piece to be published as a booklet. However, when Gareth saw the extent of the material I had available, he suggested that Honor's poem should appear in Poppyland's *Norfolk Documents* series.

I wanted to follow the route of the Yellow Caravan with paintbrush, camera and notebook. This I did, driving short distances of it at different times—although of course it would be possible to drive all 120 miles of the route in one day that took three young ladies two weeks in a horse-drawn vehicle. In the summer of 2019, I did the route again with one of Honor's great nephews Ben Elwes, a professional photographer, taking contemporary photographs of the route and the camping sites of 1912. It took six days to capture the superb scenery of the journey. During my research into the trip I bothered a great many people and asked a lot of questions. I was delighted and surprised by the varied answers and information so kindly and generously given. Keeping to the route as described by Honor, more up to date information has been added as an aide, but by no means a comprehensive one, for today's visitor. The roads of one hundred years ago have altered a great deal in the time that has passed. Most of the roads at that time were simply double tracks with grass growing down the middle. Consulting Ordnance Survey maps available for Norfolk in 1912—on a scale two miles to the inch—it has not always been possible to make out the exact route The Yellow Caravan took on its scenic journey round some of Norfolk's best loved places. Today the route is crossed by wider, faster, straighter, but not necessarily prettier, roads. If following the route, on approaching a junction where there is some doubt—take the straightest line and it will likely be the correct one! The old-fashioned wooden signposts are very useful—but there is little call for sat-nav on this journey and most reflective metal directional signs and fast roads can be ignored.

Anyone making a similar journey today is sure to be well rewarded but to get the best out of it a five-day trip would be the absolute minimum. The route advised by Christopher (Christo) Birkbeck takes our heroines through the scenery of North Norfolk and its coastline (now recognised as an Area of Outstanding Natural Beauty) the Broads, the secret scenery of South Norfolk and the wide-open spaces of Breckland. At the end of the book is a list of suggested existing camp sites. One good way of seeing the North Norfolk landscape today (albeit with a great deal of modern traffic) is to take advantage of the Coast Hopper bus (on the Wells to Cromer section of the journey) or even to walk a section of the Norfolk Coastal Path. The Broads have few camp sites, but better by far is to *hire a boat and get afloat* to be *happy as can be* as our heroines did. These three young women, on their 15 nights away from home, spent two nights at three different places (Kelling Heath, Northrepps Wood and Dunston Common) otherwise they move on each morning when Mr Canham and the horse regularly appear at 9.00 a.m.

I have been unable to trace any relatives of Mr Canham who was one of the main characters involved on the trip and undertook an important role in the story. He was clearly trusted and valued by the young women's parents and the journey could not have been made without him.

There were few motor vehicles on country roads in 1912, at a time when the speed limit was 20 mph. Roads tended to all look the same, with few milestones—and none were numbered. Although a road tax had been created in 1909 and a year later action taken to upgrade roads, a numbering system was not introduced until the 1920s.

Following the good Norfolk tradition "when in doubt, swallow it" given below is the true Norfolk pronunciation for some place names on The Yellow Caravan route that are occasionally mispronounced by visitors. These should be: "Snet-sham" for Snettisham, "Hole-kum" for Holkham; Blakeney should be pronounced "Blake-Ni", "Cly" for Cley, "Webbern" for Weybourne , "North-rups" for Northrepps, "Small-bruh" for Smallborough, "Neets-tid" for Neatishead, and when you have crossed the Bure and see signs to Salhouse don't think you are back on the North Norfolk Coast at Salthouse: this one is pronounced "Sal-uss". Postwick is pronounced "Pozzick", and Wymondham is "Wind-um" and on the home stretch, Narborough should be pronounced "Nar-bruh". In addition to all the above, some hard-liners say "Stew-key" for Stiffkey and "Por-land" for Poringland, although I do not.

As an enthusiastic amateur writer and lover of my native county, I have found the opportunity to write about Norfolk in the present day a very rewarding exercise. It was something I had not done for 70 years since penning *My Book of the Broads* (a yellow hand-made paper-back single copy no longer in existence). I hope that readers of The Yellow Caravan will have as much pleasure as I have following the route taken in 1912. It has also given me the chance to draw on my library of Norfolk books, still a considerable number, despite having given away a large selection when Mr Hilary Hammond, the Director of the Norfolk Library Services, appealed for gifts of Norfolk books after the devastating fire at Norwich Central Library in August 1994.

It is appropriate that *The Yellow Caravan* is being published in the year Anglia Television celebrates its Diamond Anniversary. I joined the typing pool, earning £5 a week, eighteen months after Anglia first went on air (28th October 1959). There I met and formed a mutual admiration society with Dick Joice and twice appeared with him on his programme *Bygones*. Dick was inspirational about Norfolk and its rural past and he would have enjoyed *The Yellow Caravan* enormously. His widow Jean has been a great encouragement to me since I first discovered the story almost twenty years ago.

Never give up!

Juliet Webster, 2019

Introduction

There are 650 villages in Norfolk. In the summer of 1912, The Yellow Caravan with its travellers visited 54 of them in two consecutive weeks. Honora (Honor) Elwes was a great enthusiast for her native Norfolk and the trip she made with her sister Winifred (Win) Elwes and her cousin Judith (Judse) Birkbeck in the summer of 1912 made a lasting impression on her—not only did she write a diary every evening of the trip, but on returning to her home at Congham, she settled down and composed a lengthy poem on the journey. We have no evidence that she ever published the poem, although written in pencil in a different hand on the fly leaf of her beautifully presented sixteen-page manuscript is a note: *three copies type written 8vo book half cloth and corners drop paper red* is an indication that Honor at one stage had intended her Norfolk Ballad to be read more widely.

My mother, Susan Elwes, had two aunts of whom she was immensely fond, and because of her own mother's untimely death, when Susan was 10 years old, her father's sisters, Honor and Win Elwes, featured a great deal in my mother's life. But the story of this journey round Norfolk in 1912 takes place three years before my mother was even born when Honor and Win were 23 and 20.

Honor and Win spent their early childhood in Congham House near Kings Lynn, a large country house belonging to their father Arthur Elwes. In 1907 Arthur Elwes died suddenly and his children and their widowed mother, Millicent Elwes, moved to Little Congham, a Georgian farmhouse nearby on the Hillington Road. Honor and Win were educated at home by a governess, and, together with their younger brother Godfrey, they had thought up and written many stories

Honor Elwes aged 22.

together. Honor was the scribe of the trio and she longed to be recognised as a writer. Sadly, Congham House was destroyed by fire in November 1939 and was never rebuilt.

Win was the practical one. She was interested in engines and mechanics and had learnt carpentry under the watchful eye of William Driver, the Congham estate carpenter, making, amongst other pieces, a small chest of drawers in oak which she kept with her all her life. Her skills in carpentry were later to come in very useful when, as a Voluntary Aid Detachment (VAD) Ambulance Driver in France during the First World War, Win made the shelves and cupboards for her Nissen Hut.

Win Elwes aged 19.

Honor loved her native Norfolk, its highways and byways, heaths, marshes and streams. The muscle-wasting disability from which she had suffered since childhood, gave rise to her nickname 'Painy'. Despite this, Honor was full of good works around Congham, Roydon, Pott Row and Grimston. She was a frequent visitor to the school, organised cricket matches and fetes for the Red Cross and raised money for local good works. The Girl Guide movement started in England in 1910 and quickly gathered momentum. Honor was extremely interested in this and ran camps for local Cubs and Girl Guides. She loved children and wrote animal and fairy stories creating characters in her head placing them in the fields, woods, marshes and streams by which she was surrounded. The names Honor invented mimicked their sounds or their appearance: 'Flash-o-Light' the Kingfisher, 'Scurry' the Partridge, 'Cooey' the Pigeon and 'Swimswift' the Trout, to mention a few.

At Little Congham Honor's mother Millicent Elwes had a number of people living in to assist with the running of the household. She had a lady's maid, Miss Mary Dance, as well as a cook, parlour maid, housemaid and under-girl but none-the-less, Honor and Win could turn their hands to anything. The footman lived in the next village, Hillington.

Win and Honor had three Elwes aunts living in the district: 'Aunt La' (Miss

Honor and Ted Smith mowing the lawn at Little Congham.

Violet Elwes) who lived at Elder Farm, Grimston; 'Aunt Milly', Lady ffolkes, living at Hillington and 'Aunt Ysabel', married to Henry Birkbeck at Westacre High House, who is referred to as 'HB'. Living nearby to their cousins, the Elwes, ffolkes and Birkbeck families were frequent visitors to one another's houses. Congham was within walking distance of Grimston and Hillington and a short ride by pony and trap to Westacre. Ysabel and HB's children at Westacre High House were first cousins to Honor and Win and they were also affectionate friends. Four of the young Birkbecks feature in this story: Harry, the eldest (aged 28), already married in February 1912 to Sybil was in the Norfolk Yeomanry; Gervase,

Christo Birkbeck aged 23.

age 27 (nicknamed 'Garvee') worked in Barclays Bank in Kings Lynn and Christopher (Christo, aged 23) a land agent, not only knew Norfolk well but, knew other land agents around the county. It was Christo who had mainly devised the route the Yellow Caravan should take. Their sister Judith (25, nicknamed Judse) accompanied Honor and Win on this trip.

Judith was regarded as the leader of this pack of three, being a more experienced traveller. Four years earlier, in 1908, Judith had visited her older sister, Gillian (Gillie) Barclay, married to a missionary in Japan. Gillie had sadly died of septicaemia three months after

Judse Birkbeck aged 24.

giving birth to a baby son. Judith, with her younger sister and her mother, had travelled out to Japan to visit Gillie, sailing via Ceylon and China, and returned across the Pacific and Canada bringing Gillie's new baby, Roddy Barclay, home with them.

The Elwes gang were high spirited and adventurous but their mothers had obviously given permission for the young women to go on this trip which had taken them a great deal of time and letter-writing to arrange. There is something very poignant about this adventure: although they were still very young, for them it was perhaps representative of teenage freedom but with hindsight could be regarded now as something of a 'last fling' for our three heroines, because two years later, life would change for ever with the outbreak of the First World War in which they were to lose so many who were dear to them (see Postscript).

Carefully chosen by the mothers, Millicent Elwes and Ysabel Birkbeck, to accompany the young ladies on the two-week trip round the county, was Charlie Canham who was acting as groom for the journey looking after and leading the horse. The mothers would certainly not have given permission for such an expedition unless there was someone accompanying the trio whom they trusted implicitly. Charlie Canham was the man. Listed in the 1911 Census as a "Watercress Carman" at Westacre Mr Canham, although born in Essex, came from a Norfolk family. His father was from West Bradenham and was closely related to Mrs William Coe of West Acre—the former Mary Anne Canham from

West Bradenham. When they were married, Mr & Mrs Coe moved from West Bradenham to look after the garden at West Acre. In 1901, at the age of 19 Charlie Canham, Mrs Coe's nephew, had enlisted in the Royal Marines Light Infantry and his reports from there were exemplary. On leaving the Marines he came to Norfolk and lived with the Coe family at Westacre to look after the Watercress beds. In the autumn of 1911, at the age of 29 Charlie Canham married Ellen Coe, who was working nearby as a dressmaker for the Turner family at the Manor House, West Bilney. So, a newly married former Royal Marine with a first-class record, who had been looking after horses and carts on the estate and was related to their gardener's wife, would be an ideal choice of travelling supervisor and companion for the three young ladies on their trip of a lifetime.

Charlie Canham.

The Westacre watercress farm industry was considerable. Mr Thomas Fryer who lived at The Mill House in Westacre managed the farming of the watercress. The natural springs that bubbled up through the chalk created shallow running water in a series of ponds, perfect conditions for growing watercress. Watercress had to be cut, bunched and packed in wicker baskets and then transported by horse and cart to Narborough Station and thence to London.[1]

So it was a change for Charlie Canham from the constant carting of watercress from Westacre to Narborough, to be asked to accompany three young ladies on a two-week tour round Norfolk, his father's native county. On the journey Canham would be up early. He needed to feed the horse two hours before it started working. The rented horse was not a fat horse, but all horses then were working animals and they were fit. Having fed and watered the horse, Canham then had to get himself ready and well turned out in his stiff collar and tie, waistcoat, tweeds and over his leather shoes his highly polished brown leather gaiters buckled just below the knee. After his breakfast he would brush the horse down, check and harness it with bridle, blinkers, girth, traces, breeching strap, reins and collar. Cart-horse collars came in different sizes and each had to fit the

---

1 *The Westacre Watercress business was killed off by the hard winter of 1963 when the watercress was all dug out, exposing the many natural springs. Its place was later taken by the Westacre Trout Farm which started in 1964.*

horse exactly in order that the animal could use its full weight and strength without the collar chaffing in any way. A perfectionist might say that a carthorse does not pull, it pushes. It pushes its chest into the perfectly fitting collar. The breeching strap round the hind quarters allowed the horse to lean back on a downward incline.

The traces were straps of leather reaching from the horse's collar to the load which went tight on an upward slope and would slacken on the downward slope. When the horse came out of the shafts, the traces were folded or rolled up in a coil. In the Hingham photograph[2], the traces are dangling on the ground from the collar.

The Yellow Caravan with Honor, Win and Judse with dogs Kaiser and Seizer.

The journey round Norfolk was made at walking pace most of the time. The Yellow Caravan would have weighed approximately a ton and a quarter. There was no drag on a wooden cartwheel with an iron tyre, it would roll well on the flat—unlike a rubber tyre that has a grip. Once the van had momentum, it would roll itself on level ground and only need the very minimum of strength to propel it forward.

The horse may have trotted in places when the ground was level, and uphill it would need to trot hard to get momentum to negotiate the incline. When Charlie Canham drove the horse he would have the long reins in his left hand. He may even have had to use his driving whip on a steep hill. The whip would live on the shelf next to where he sat. He would be sitting on the shelf, talking to the horse or singing to it to encourage it on its way. Charlie Canham's right hand would be free for the brake which he would apply when going downhill. The brake was a little wheel with three spokes and a small handle (similar to a vintage sewing machine handle). This operated a long rod with a coarse winding thread that pushed small blocks of wood against the back wheels. Normally, the brake blocks would be on the front edges of the rear wheels of a wagon, but the Yellow Caravan had the brake blocks on the back edges.

For possibly as much as half the journey, Charlie Canham may have walked or

2 page 115.

trotted with the horse. He would be on the left side of the horse, with the reins in his left hand, so that his right hand was near the brake. The girls too would have walked, and certainly when going up a hill the girls would be walking behind the caravan. When they rode, there would be room for one on the shelf with Charlie Canham, and another may have sat on a stool in the open doorway. But it was raining most of the time!

When the party stopped at mid-day for their own lunch, Canham had a flask that hung under the caravan and the horse was fed from a nosebag which was also slung underneath: a supply of corn would be carried on board. The horse would also need about half a bucket of water at mid-day, if there was not a nearby convenient stream for it to drink from. Water may have lived inside the caravan in a churn. Horsemen liked churns for travelling as they had a good secure lid which would prevent the water sloshing out.

In the evening, Canham would unharness the horse, brush every inch of it and check it over for sores in case the harness had chafed. The harness itself would need to be cleaned and oiled at least twice on the journey. He would feed the horse and give it as much water as it wanted. He would check its feet and shoes. A set of new shoes is likely to have lasted the whole 120 miles of the journey. If there was a problem with the harness, such as a broken buckle, he would need to attend to that. The harness would be saturated with sweat and rain and needed to be put in the air under cover to dry. Canham would only have the minimum of equipment with him, so if there was a bigger problem with the harness, he would have to get that attended to by a harness maker. Most villages had one, in addition to a village blacksmith.

Honor never mentions the sleeping arrangements for Canham: it is likely he would be sleeping near the horse, possibly in the hayloft above the stall where the horse was stabled for the night. He would not have been very far from the Yellow Caravan, as the girls' parents would be expecting him to act as a discreet sentinel for them. Although it is uncertain how this worked in a remote spot like Kelling Heath.

Trenowath and Son business card.

This photograph reveals the Yellow Caravan's origins—one of a pair of travelling Bioscope wagons. The ticket window can be seen next to the door at the left hand side of the caravan.

The caravan they hired from Mr Trenowath in Kings Lynn was not a gypsy caravan. It was a steep sided rectangular box—mounted on a flat cart with wooden wheels. It was once one of a pair of Bioscope wagons forming the front to a travelling show, which when erected had behind it a tented auditorium. Many of these bioscope wagons were made by Orton & Co. of Burton on Trent. By 1912 travelling show wagons were being phased out as Assembly Rooms and cinemas were starting to be built in towns. When on the move, the top boards of the wagons were folded down. The plain sides were painted in colour advertising 'What's On'—although the real attraction was the technology itself of these early cinemas.

When it was a bioscope wagon, the public came up the steps and paid their money at a little window before descending into the auditorium on the other side. Inside the van there may have been a safe in the cupboard below the window. We know the van was *big and roomy* and that it had a coal-burning stove inside with a chimney going up through the roof. The three young women had one hundredweight of coal with them for fuel for the journey.

There was also a cupboard in the van they nick-named the 'C.T.' cupboard which leaked every time it rained. When Win opened the cupboard door she

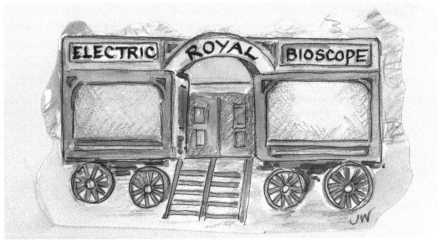

Drawing of how the Bioscope wagons formed the entrance to the show.

would say "Curse Trenny"—C.T.[3].

The Trenowath family were originally mariners from Cornwall where their name was pronounced "Tren-o-ath" and they arrived in Lynn from the sea. The first Mr Trenowath established a silk business in Lynn trading with the Far East. By the early 1900's, three of his descendants had separate businesses in Lynn: Walter, Tomson and Arthur. Walter Trenowath, whom Honor refers to as "Trenny" in the diary, traded in the High Street and also ran a cabinet-making and general furniture business. Later Trenny added furniture removal, undertaking, tent-making & contracting whilst his two brothers both had general drapery businesses.

Handsome Walter Trenowath, "Trenny", was described as "a bit of a lad" and something of a ladies man, but nonetheless the business held a Royal Appointment to HM King Edward VII and Queen Alexandra. When the Royal Family ceased to live at Osborne House, Trenny, who was known to spend a lot of time at Sandringham, organised the furniture removal there for Her Majesty the Queen from the Isle of Wight. Trenny's vehicles included a pantechnicon as well as horse-drawn wagons.

Walter Trenowath.

3 *Trenny was Mr Trenowath.*

The Trenowath family lived at Ouse House on Purfleet Quay in Lynn. The Trenowath horses were kept in stables in the yard of the same name running down to the Quay from 11 King Street. Trenowath horses also pulled the town fire engine. The fire engine appliance itself, however, was housed at the back of the then Barclays Bank behind Tuesday Market Place. In the event of a fire, Trenowath's white horses were rushed to the back of the Bank.

The Trenowath family would exercise their horses riding out to Massingham Heath and back to Lynn before breakfast. Camping, too, was nothing to Trenny who took the whole family in his pantechnicon loaded with a marquee, carpets, household furniture, beds, dining table and the rest and they set up camp in the marquee pitched at

Home Farm in North Wootton, Trenny's "house in the country" where he kept horses and wagons, 2019.

Heacham for the family seaside holiday. The Trenowath family also had a house at Home Farm, North Wootton, where the family would visit for a holiday in the country. Trenny kept more horses and wagons at North Wootton which is why Honor, Win and Judith start their Norfolk adventure from there.

In May 1912, Sir George White, the sitting Liberal Member of Parliament for North West Norfolk since 1900, had died whilst in office and his funeral had taken place in Norwich attended by a record number of mourners, something over 3,000 people. In his lifetime, Sir George White had founded the shoe manufacturers Hewlett & White, which later became the Norvic Shoe Company.

And so it was from Trenny's stables at North Wootton that Honor, Win and Judith commenced their circular journey round Norfolk from the constituency that had recently lost its MP.

At that time the Suffragettes were campaigning in North West Norfolk for Edward Hemmerede, the Liberal Candidate standing against Neville Jodrell, Conservative. Just a few miles away in Kings Lynn, elegant hats were being worn by ladies in the High Street that day decorated in the colours of the Women's Suffrage Movement: Green, White & Violet G-W-V (Give Women the Vote). With an 80% turnout, the result of the election was that the Liberals were returned. Aunt Violet in her diary wrote, *N.W.N. Poll. Hemmerede in though Mr Joddrell has brought the majority down 600—pretty good!*

Kaiser & Seizer were the two faithful dogs who accompany the party all round

Norfolk. Kaiser was the black flat-coated Labrador, and Seizer the West Highland Terrier. Whether it is Honor's spelling that is at fault and his name is meant to be 'Caesar' is unclear, but Seizer is a rather bizarre name for a dog. Their former neighbour at Sandringham, King Edward VII had a Norfolk Terrier named Caesar to whom the King was devoted. Honor may have had the opportunity of meeting the royal terrier 'Caesar' as King Edward VII had once been a familiar figure shooting at Congham with Honor's father and Honor may have taken a fancy to the name.

How the inside of the caravan might have looked based on Mrs Zigamala's sketches.

From the text of Honor's diary we learn little of the inside of the van. However, a sketch made later that same year, when the Zigamala family (pronounced Zigama-La) took the same lemon-yellow van in a convoy of two, tells us more. Mrs Zigamala (the former Miss Hilda North a member of the very artistic and talented family from Rougham) made a sketch of "Tired Caravaners" two girls asleep in all their clothes on the top double bunk which is level with the little curtained window of the van. Mrs Zigamala's photographs suggest there is another double bunk below. A curtain pulled across the middle of the van affords the sleepers a little privacy. The best insight however, into how the interior could have been fitted out, is a description of Toad's caravan in *The Wind in the Willows*, written by Kenneth Grahame four years earlier in 1908. Toad leads the way to the stable-yard…

and there, drawn out of the coach-house into the open, they saw a gipsy caravan, shining with newness, painted a canary-yellow with red wheels. "There you are!" cried Toad, "There's real life for you, embodied in that little cart. The open road, the dusty highway, the heath, the common, the hedgerows, the rolling downs! Camps, villages, towns, cities! Here to-day, up and off to somewhere else to-morrow! Travel, chance, interest, excitement! The whole world before you and a horizon that's always changing! And mind, this is the finest cart of its sort that was ever built, without any exception." Inside it was very compact and comfortable. Little sleeping-bunks—a little table that folded up against the wall—a cooking-stove, lockers, bookshelves, a bird-cage with a bird in it; and pots, pans, jugs and kettles of every size and variety. "All complete!" said Toad triumphantly, pulling open a locker. "You see—biscuits, potted lobster, sardines—everything you can possibly want. Soda-water here—baccy there—letter-paper, bacon, jam, cards and dominos. We'll make our start this afternoon... .

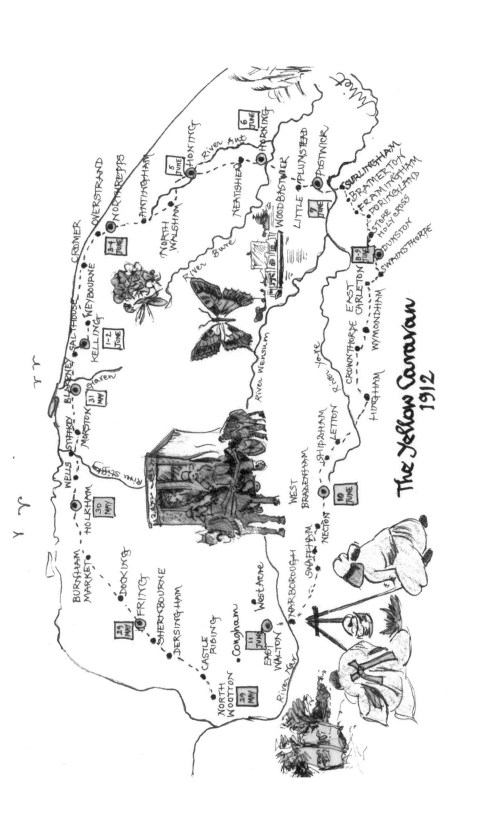

The Yellow Caravan
1912

DAY ONE

Mistaken for Suffragettes

Wednesday 29ᵀᴴ May 1912
North Wootton to Fring (11 miles) via Castle Rising, Babingley,
Sandringham Woods, Shernbourne and Dersingham

We started from North Wootton
On the twenty-ninth of May
With Caravan and horse and man
All ready for the fray.

We were all lending helping hands
While the packing was being done,
They dropped the coals upon Win's foot,
"Accident Number One".

The van was packed by maid and man
Who cheered to see us go,
The butter had been left behind
But this we did not know
Till the footman caught us up with it
On the road a mile or so!

A little party of well-wishers had gathered at Home Farm, North Wootton, where Trenny kept horses and vehicles. Honor and Win had driven the six miles from Little Congham in the pony cart. Ted Smith—who helped out at Little Congham with tasks such as the lawn mowing that he shared with Win—followed with the luggage in the luggage cart. This was full to overflowing with supplies for the two-week tour round Norfolk. Whether Trenny had supplied the canvas deck chairs and a tea chest we can only guess. The deck chairs were of the folding wooden rectangular type slung with one piece of canvas, easy to fold and move around (800 identical chairs had been swept into the North Atlantic from the deck of the Titanic only six weeks earlier). Two ladders were supplied, one long

Honor & Judith having breakfast

This captioned photo in Honor's album shows the deck chairs and Harrods' tea-chest used to provide seating and a camp table.

enough for them to access the roof on which to store the folding chairs, which were then covered with a waterproof cloth. A short ladder was also supplied for the travellers to reach the doorway. The Harrods' tea chest is a bit of a mystery. Neither the Congham household nor the Westacre household would have had their tea delivered in chests from Harrods of Knightsbridge. Tea was indeed delivered to both households in thin wooden chests with riveted metal edges and lined with foil but their tea would have come direct from Ceylon where the Elwes family had tea estates. Honor and Win's uncle Dick Elwes had been sent out there at the age of 16 in April 1886 to look after the family tea business and continued to do so well into his 80s. Later, Honor was fortunate enough to visit him in Ceylon three times and kept a diary of her visits. For the Yellow Caravan trip, it is likely that Trenny, being in the house removals business, supplied the tea chest. Trenny may even have acquired it from Queen Alexandra when he moved her possessions about. The Royal Household may well have had their tea delivered from Harrods. Trenny would have had plenty of tea chests for packing and he probably also supplied the basic pots and pans as well as the cauldron and its tripod—as Trenny we know was something of a happy camper himself and well aware of what would be needed for the two-week journey.

By the time Honor and Win arrived at North Wootton, Judith Birkbeck was already at Home Farm with her mother who had arrived from Westacre with her lady's maid Edith Goymer. Both were waiting to see the Yellow Caravan depart. Honor's Aunt Violet had also arrived from Elder Farm, Grimston, to see the fun. Aunt Violet wrote in her diary that evening:

> *Went to Wootton to see Honor, Win and Judes start on a fortnight's caravan trip. They did look so happy and the caravan very big and roomy.*

It took time to unpack both luggage carts and re-stow everything neatly into the Yellow Caravan. The only accident that morning was Ted Smith dropping the hundredweight (8 stone or 50 kg) sack of coal on Win's foot. It was a quarter to twelve before they left with Charlie Canham leading the horse. *The van was packed by maid and man who cheered to see us go.* Despite the number of helpers, the butter was left out, but Ted Smith ran with it and caught them up on the road before they had gone too far.

The Village Green, North Wootton, where Honor, Win and Judse started their journey around Norfolk, 2019.

The journey starts on the village green at North Wootton by the red telephone box opposite Home Farm—thence turning right along Ling Common Road. Here rural Norfolk begins with tall trees on either side of the road which continue all the way to Castle Rising. Castle Rising was a place so familiar to Honor living nearby at Congham that she does not mention it in poem or diary. Today the village of Castle Rising is beautifully kept and it is a joy to visit—walls, houses and churches here are built in local carstone[1]. First time visitors to Castle Rising feel immediately that they have arrived somewhere quite different. The church with carstone walls and Romanesque roofed tower is by no means a typical Norfolk

---

1 *Carstone is rusty ginger coloured sandstone that extends in a narrow strip northwards to the coast at Hunstanton where it becomes visible in the face of the cliffs below a layer of chalk.*

church and, on the opposite side of the road, the Trinity Hospital alms houses, also in carstone, are intriguing. They were built in the reign of King James I by the Howards whose family have resided here since Castle Rising was built in the 12th century. Down a side-road it is possible to catch a glimpse of the great Norman mound of Castle Rising Castle, cared for today by English Heritage. One of the finest stone keeps in Britain is surrounded by 20 acres of massive earthworks. In the centre of the village are cottage garden tea rooms serving coffees, lunches and teas in delightful surroundings.

The Yellow Caravan party stopped for lunch on the road between Babingley and Wolferton. Babingley, a hamlet on the Sandringham Estate, is named after the 12-mile long Babingley river that rises in 'Further Back Wood' in Flitcham, and is joined by the even smaller Cong River rising in Congham. Honor does not mention Sandringham by name (but stopping between Babingley and Wolferton tells us she is at Sandringham). Their journey took them through the wonderful woods of Sandringham and past the 'Norwich Gates' of the Royal residence. Today the Sandringham Estate has beautifully equipped camp sites for caravans and tents located in spectacular woodland. The Sandringham Country Park has pathways and walks through the woods and an exceptional visitor centre and gift shop and a restaurant offering

Sandringham Woods, 2019.

first-class meals and service. There is also a museum of royal memorabilia and vehicles. When Honor, Win and Judith stopped nearby for their lunch, they could never have envisaged such wonderful facilities 100 years on or imagined that the journey they had embarked on would be emulated in part by so many thousands of visitors to the county.

Wolferton was the royal station—not exactly on the route, but visitors may want to take a short detour. Between 1862 and 1969 the Royal Train brought members of the Royal Family and their guests here on their journeys to Sandringham. It is now a station without a track and has been lovingly restored as a private house.

Us, on the road. Win
Judse, Canham
a Sisson

Fring was our destination
So we hurried on ahead
And past thu' Dersingham and bought
Our first new loaf of bread.

Through Snettisham village, to the right,
And up a short steep hill,
Canham, the man, persuades the horse
While we pushed with a will.

Dersingham Bog, on the Sandringham Estate, today has open access and
there are many intriguing, well-marked walks through heather, Corsican pines
with silver birch trees glinting in between. It is a Site of Special Scientific Interest
and consists of waterlogged peat, woodland and a ridge of dry heath. It is a good

place to wander in.

At the time the Yellow Caravan visited Dersingham, the village had four butchers and three bakers—so we cannot tell whether the Yellow Caravan party purchased their first loaf from Mr Jarvis, James Fitt or Herbert Playford—the latter being a baker and confectioner holding the Royal Warrant.

Although Honor mentions Snettisham in her poem (though not in her diary) it is likely that they took the more direct route from Dersingham to Fring, through Shernbourne (the name means 'Muddy Stream') another village on the Sandringham Estate. As their mode of travel was slow, they would not have had time to visit the church of St. Peter and St. Paul which comes into view at the foot of a hill. This hill marks the eastern edge of the carstone ridge, so the church here at Shernbourne is built of local flint. Within it is a gem of a thousand years old. In this corner of Norfolk there are twenty churches with carved Norman fonts, and, in the opinion of the experts, Shernbourne holds the finest one of them. Stop and admire this Norfolk treasure!

Sherbourne church coming into view, 2019.

> **As Fring approached us with the eve**
> **A thunder storm past by**
> **But by the time we'd got a field**
> **The sun shone out on high.**
>
> **Judith and Win with Siezer dog**
> **Soon found the farmer man**
> **Who said "What are you? Suffragettes,?**
> **If not, camp here you can."**
>
> **We raised the awning, pitched the tent,**
> **And soon the fire was lit,**
> **And on the top of all the sticks**
> **The kettle tried to sit.**
>
> **Asparagus, potatoes fried,**
> **Poached eggs and cocoa hot,**
> **Was our first meal, then we put on**

Caully, the water pot.

Honor wrote in her diary:

We then pushed on to Fring which was a good long way. There was a heavy shower before we arrived at Fring. We found an awfully nice farm and the farmer said we certainly might camp there provided we weren't Suffragettes or anything political! (The Suffragettes are about owing to the by-election). We made an outside fire and cooked our dinner of poached eggs, asparagus and fried potatoes on it. Kaiser and Siezer never barked all night.

Fring, like many small Norfolk villages, in 1912 had a population totally dependent on farming. Apart from the Schoolmistress, one General Dealer and one "Police Pensioner/Beer House keeper" there were 33 men working as general farm labourers in Fring. In addition, there were six men working as Teamsmen (who drove the teams of horses) six horsemen, four grooms, three yardmen, two gardeners, two shepherds, one retired shepherd, a stock feeder and a game-keeper. Besides the two farm bailiffs, there were two farmers living in Fring—one at Church Farm and the other at The White House. It is fairly obvious the Yellow Caravan called at Church Farm—easy to pull off the road there—and the girls would have spoken to either Mr Archie Coe or his son Henry who, having established they were not *suffragettes or anything political*, gave them permission to camp in a field that first night.

Church Farm, Fring, 2019.

After each meal 'Caully Cauldron' the water-pot was attached to a wrought-iron tripod known as a 'Kettle Iron' and was placed over the centre of the camp fire where the heat was greatest. This would provide them not only with washing up water, but water for their own ablutions. The striped tent, provided by Trenny, was pitched each time the Yellow Caravan stopped for the night. This was quite a large tent and the young ladies would use it as their place to wash in. There would also be a hole dug in the ground there, filled in by Canham every morning before moving off.

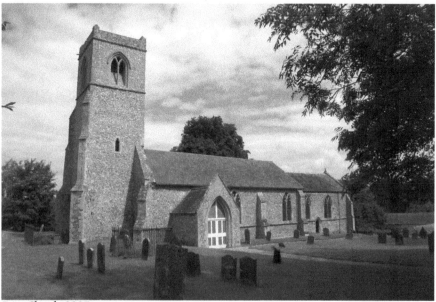

Fring Church, 2007.

Fring nestles in the hollow of narrow Norfolk lanes where the ancient track, Peddars Way, continues on its straight path in a north-westerly direction to the coast. Standing on rising ground, looking down on Church Farm, is the 14th century church of All Saints. Inside, opposite the south door, is a fifteen foot high fresco of Saint Christopher, the patron saint of travellers, painted around 1330. This is most appropriate as medieval journeymen used the pre-Roman highway on which Fring stands. Its presence near the start of the 1912 journey bodes well for travellers both ancient and modern. Honor, Win and Judith were able to camp their first night in a field in Fring, but today, if you were wishing to stay in this particular village, the Fring Estate have holiday cottages for rent and offer their holidaymakers bicycles to hire during visits. Cycling the 11 miles from Fring to Castle Rising via Sandringham, Dersingham Bog and Shernbourne and back, would make a wonderful day out with plenty to see and do.

When Caully Cauldron boiled, and we
Had washed up every plate
While a cuckoo cucked we went to bed
Because 't'was getting late.

The young ladies end their first day while the cuckoo is still calling:

In April I ope' my bill; in May I sing all day; in June I change my tune; in July away I fly, in August go I must.

DAY TWO

A Bouquet of Wild Flowers from Friars Thorn Farm

Thursday 30th May 1912
Fring to Holkham (15 miles) via Docking and Burnham Market

The sun arose and so did we,
And breakfast soon was laid
Bacon and eggs soon sizzled loud
The tea was quickly made.

The tent was then placed on the top,
The pots were placed below,
Kaiser and Siezer ran beneath
And we all forward go.

Honor wrote in her diary:

Got up between 6.30 and 7.00. Had a good breakfast of fried bacon and scrambled eggs, cooked outside. We shall always use the outside fire if we can and can get dry kindling. We heat all our washing up water on the caldron over the fire hanging on a tripod. Canham and the horse turned up at 9.00 and we got off at 9.30. It was all uphill from Fring to Docking which was rather hard on the horse. We loafed about Docking getting a few things we wanted. Our two new pails wanted soldering which Canham got done for 2d. One old man asked me if we were a travelling show as some of them came to Docking!

At Docking on an awful hill
A blacksmith mends our pails with lead,
"Shall I mend them well enough
For you to sell again?" he said.

The undulating road is a delight to drive in the 21st century and, although an uphill pull for the horse and caravan, the landscape here would have been a joy to the young ladies one hundred years ago, even in the rain. However, it would have been a relief for them to arrive in Docking. In 1912 there were three blacksmiths in Docking as well as a harness maker. Today, in the centre

The Old Smithy at Docking, 2019.

of the village just south of the village pond, an unmistakable former blacksmith's forge can still be seen. When the young ladies' bucket is mended by the blacksmith in Docking, he assumed that the girls were tinkers. Tinkers were travelling people who did seasonal work on farms. By tradition they repaired pots and pans and made willow baskets and clothes-pegs for their womenfolk to sell. In addition, many tinkers dealt in scrap iron.

Docking today has an excellent village shop and post office and a weekly market offering local produce. The Railway Inn, although no longer serving a railway, is now the only pub in the village. Both the former pubs 'The Hare' and the 'King William IV' have now become private housing. There is no camp site, but luxury cottages are available to rent in the village.

We lunched e'er Burnham hove in sight
Up another hill so steep,
Canham drew water from a well
Three hundred footer deep!

We stopped to get water at a farm just before lunch. The well was 287 ft. deep. A small boy gave us a big bunch of flowers which later on upset over Canham's coat when the horse stopped with a jerk. We lunched on the road three miles before Burnham. We had such a feast. Judse made some oxtail soup and we still had some cold lamb and Judse had made a cornflour shape in the morning, so that was cold, and then we had some boiled potatoes and cucumber and lettuce and bread and butter, and lemonade.

In 1912 four farming families lived at Friars Thorn Farm, three miles short of Burnham Market, but today only one farmhouse and one cottage remain. The deep well behind the farmhouse was filled in around the year 2000. In the farmyard stands an impressive barn of Norfolk 'clunch'—chalk blocks embedded with gritty broken shells. Heightened at one stage with additional rows of flint, the barn has an unusual and attractive brick archway. In 1912 George Purdy the farm bailiff was living at Friars Thorn, as were the Clarke, Grief and Rout

Friars Thorn Farm between Docking & Burnham Market once had a deep well behind the house, 2019.

families, all with young children. If the boys were all attending school, as they should have been, it only left young Isaac Grief (whose father was the Teamster, looking after the Friars Thorn horses), aged about 4½ at the time, to be the small boy who presented the young ladies with a big bunch of flowers when they stopped for water there. But why did they choose to stop at this particular farm for water and not at a well in Docking—where admittedly they would have been charged a farthing for a pail of water? And was there any significance to the presentation of the big bunch of flowers? For strangers to be greeted thus, in a vacant and lonely place, seems rather unusual for shy Norfolk people. It is perfectly believable that the Grief family at Friars Thorn were forewarned that the Yellow Caravan and its occupants were expected. They may have been related to the Grief family who lived at Congham— Honor and Win's village. Or perhaps Charlie Canham knew of the family and was heading for Friars Thorn aware they had a well. The nearest school for Friars Thorn, which was situated in Burnham Westgate parish, was three miles further on in Burnham Market.

The school stood in North Street, Burnham Market, occupying a notable narrow cobbled building behind railings. Many years later the building became the National Westminster Bank and is currently the home of North Street Bistro, 2011.

Honor was keen about her wildflowers and later in her diary mentions several species she collects for her flower book. *Bentham & Hooker's Handbook of British Flora*, first published in 1862 with many subsequent editions, was regarded as the authority on British wildflowers for many generations. The book had no illustrations until in 1887 a companion volume by Fitch and Smith *Illustrations of the British Flora* became available. This was not only a very desirable tome but essential for those interested in the wildflowers of Britain. Ladies with a certain amount of time and inclination would search out wildflowers, pick a specimen, take it home and paint the colours straight on to the relevant page of their Fitch and Smith. The black and white line illustrations were quite small, four specimens to a page, but it made an ideal 'memory book' when the flowers were painted if date and place were added as a hand-written note.

556.   Carduus Marianus.

Milk Thistle illustrated in Finch and Smith's book and identified in Honor's diary at Stiffkey.

From Friars Thorn Farm looking towards Burnham Market and the sea with a newly planted vineyard on a south facing slope, 2019.

The *big bunch* presented to the three young ladies was likely to have been of wildflowers that happily grew on chalky meadowland in early summer (see Appendix for a list of proper names).

Time stops here. Apart from the tarmac surface on the narrow road itself, the landscape of the route is seen today very much as our heroines saw it—green and inviting. Driving down this little road from Docking to Burnham Market is a 21st century delight with sparse traffic except for the occasional cyclist. The undulating landscape disappears as the road leads through a cool, dark Long Plantation beyond which a vineyard has recently been established on a south facing slope.

Burnham Market: *London Bristol and Coven Tree and the Seven Burnhams by the Sea*. The meaning of this traditional rhyme is obscure. The Coven Tree is the Wayfaring Tree (Viburnum Lantana) a shrub with a springy stem, also known as 'Lithy Wood', 'Twist Wood' and 'Whip crop': *The carters doe make their whippes of it* (English Dialect Dictionary).

> **It poured again by Burnham**
> **So we all got inside**
> **But when we got to Holkham**
> **Our things had nearly dried,**
> **All but the chairs that we, alas**
> **Had stuck up on the roof,**
> **And covered with a cloth that we**
> **Had thought was waterproof.**

Honor hardly mentions Burnham Market at all except to record they travelled through it in a deluge of rain. It is one of Norfolk's charming Georgian towns with a central village green. Post Office, boutique shops, restaurants and coffee bars; two of the most notable being the luxury hotel with a spa 'The Hoste' made famous by the late Paul Whittome, named after Lord Nelson's local protégé Captain William Hoste; and 'Gurney's' fish shop on the green, both so popular today with visiting tourists from London and beyond.

We did 15 miles today. An awful deluge deluged at Burnham and got the chairs wet on the roof and the dogs' bed got wet in one corner. Then we went on to Holkham. We found another pleasing farmer who lent us a horse just to help pull up into a nice field for the night. The farmer's name was Hewing. Menu for Thursday night: fried eggs, cold tongue, bread and milk and cocoa.

Hoste Arms at Burnham Market, 2012.

We got leave to camp from a farmer,
Bob Hewen was his name,
And then we found we had swept off
Our chimney, in the rain,
But as we'd travelled fifteen miles
We went not back again.

In her poem, Honor names the farmer *Bob Hewen* and in her diary *Hewing*. After consulting the Archivist at Holkham in an attempt to identify the field where they camped that night, it was clear Honor, Win and Judith were right in the middle of Holkham village near the Ancient House. The Julings (probably pronounced 'U-lings' which would account for Honor's two mis-spellings) had farmed there for several generations. In 1912 Robert Julings and his wife Kate, both in their 40s, were living in the Ancient House with three school-age children. Honor and friends arriving with their wet deck-chairs did not present them with too much of a problem of drying wet canvas, and possibly the dogs' bed too, in front of their kitchen stove.

Field opposite the Ancient House where the Yellow Caravan camped their second night, 2019.

The Ancient House, Holkham village. The home of Mr and Mrs Robert Julings and their young family in 1912, 2019.

DAY THREE

Shopping in Wells High Street

Friday, 31st May 1912
Holkham to Blakeney (9 miles) via Wells, Stiffkey and Morston

We left Canham to wash up the breakfast things and went to have a look at Holkham Bay and then got off before 10.

The rain came down e'er we were up
Next morn, but ne'ertheless
We wandered down to Holham [sic] Bay
A scene of barrenness.
Though doubtless if the sun had shone
A scene we should have gazed upon.

So wide is Holkham beach that you cannot see the end of it, and glorious as it is when the sun is shining, in the rain it is a not a lot of fun unless you get under the wonderful pine trees which can act as great natural umbrellas and create good places to go for a picnic on a wet day. But Honor and friends wanted to be on their way and did not have time even to visit Holkham Hall, the privately-

Holkham Beach, 2019.

owned Palladian mansion, the seat of the Earls of Leicester. The Hall has always had open days to the public, even in the late eighteenth century before it was fully built. Then the housekeeper took visitors around and afterwards guests would be served hot chocolate! Today, before or after visiting the house, you can buy as much hot chocolate as you like and plenty more delights in Holkham's Courtyard Café.

Holkham's park is encircled by 8 miles of wall and is surrounded by many

43

thousand acres of beautiful scenery and has a lot to offer visitors. It is also possible today to hire a bike and pedal through the park or walk to the obelisk or Holkham's Great Barn or round the lake. Or hire a canoe on this stretch of water Humphrey Repton devised from an inlet of the sea. Visitors to Holkham's own Victoria Inn located at the entrance to Holkham Park receive a warm welcome whether they are calling in for a pint after a good walk on Holkham Beach, or to dine on local fare. Visitors stay at The Victoria or at the recently renovated Ancient House—although the proprietor of the Ancient House today might get a surprise if you asked to dry out your wet deck chairs or your dog's bed!

For today's campers and caravan dwellers Holkham's own Pinewoods Holiday Park is a large and well-equipped site approached from Beach Road, Wells-next-the-Sea. It is situated amongst the woodlands of Corsican pines which were planted in the 1850s to stabilize and extend the dunes towards the sea. Near to the sand-dunes the park offers visitors sites among these trees. Pinewoods has its own Beach Café which can be reached from the town by the 10¼ gauge Wells Harbour Railway, saving a mile-long walk between the town and the beach.

An appropriate reminder of the days of horse drawn wagons is a newcomer to Wells in the form of a sculpture created from steel bars and old whiskey barrels. The ten-foot high Lifeboat Horse is a monument to the lifeboat men and to the five pairs of horses that pulled the Wells Lifeboat two and a half miles to Holkham Gap at low tide or launched it into the harbour at high tide. The same horses were used to tow heavy railway trucks loading and unloading cargo from the ships at the quayside. The sculpture stands on the harbour sands where it can be seen at low tide and becomes semi-submerged as the tide comes in.

Then on we went to Blakeney
But that took all the day
Wells and Stiffkey and Morston
We passed through on the way.

In Wells we bought a meat safe
And other things galore;
And watched the loaf we'd chosen
Come out of the oven door.

We stopped in Wells for a little shopping and got a meat safe, much clamoured after by Win and also a loaf of bread which we watched come out of the oven.

From Holkham, the route the caravan took in 1912 is likely to have been down Burnt Street as far as Church Plain where there would be room for the caravan to park and turn. On inquiring at 'Walsinghams' the hardware shop in modern Staithe Street, where it might have been possible in 1912 to have

High Street, Wells in 1922. G.F Rose the Ironmonger is on the left.

bought a zinc-fronted meat safe, we were directed to a row of modern houses now occupying the site of Thurgurs Store, *China and Carpet Warehouse and Marine Store Dealer* whose premises at 55-65 High Street once faced Church Plain. It would also have been possible for the young ladies to purchase *Other things galore* in the winding High Street, far too narrow for the caravan to negotiate. Shops offering goods and services in Wells High Street in 1912 included: grocer, fruiterer and pork butcher, confectioner, provision merchant, newsagent, cycle dealer, hairdresser, draper, tailor, two dressmakers, two ironmongers, as well as tea rooms and two public houses. Today there are no commercial premises in the High Street

Wells High Street, 2019.

at all. The pretty former Georgian shop fronts are painted in carefully chosen contrasting delicate pastel shades, their former shop windows draped in equally delicate domestic net curtaining. By standing on Church Plain and looking up the empty High Street, it is not hard to imagine shoppers 100 years ago busy buying

as Win, Honor and Judith did. It could
have been from Mr Rose's Bakery on
Church Plain, almost opposite Thurgur,
that they *watched the loaf they'd chosen
come out of the oven door.* Today, running
up from the Quayside at Wells, the main
shopping street is Staithe Street where,
although it is not possible to buy a meat
safe (we did try!), there is a butcher and
a baker and *other things galore* on offer

Former baker shop, Church Plain Wells, 2019.

from busy shops in the street and elsewhere in the town. The Yellow Caravan
continued on the Stiffkey Road out of Wells, where today there is another camp
site, 'Blue Skies'.

> **Near Stiffkey I started the dumplings,**
> **(We were cooking in the van)**
> **And the rain that was pouring steadily**
> **Through the C.T. cupboard ran.**
>
> **Something went wrong with the dumplings**
> **Though they came out nice and hot,**
> **One rose, so the others couldn't**
> **But they stuck to the boiling pot.**

Just before Stiffkey they stopped for lunch:

*It was so wet we had the fire inside. I made some Norfolk dumplings, but owing
to the lid being very tight on the saucepan, they were unable to rise as they
should. But we ate them.*

*After lunch I went and had a look round Stiffkey. Hung over the wall and saw
the oldest horse in Norfolk, an uncommonly nice looking one and posted a
letter and thought it was a very nice little place. I got three flowers at Stiffkey for
my flower book. Milk Thistle, Meadow Sage and another thistle but I couldn't
make out what it was.*

Today at the Stiffkey Stores there is a letter box, but the Victorian cast-iron one
used by Honor has been replaced by a 'lamp box style' box with an EIIR cypher.
(To take advantage of the oldest letterbox in Norfolk it would be necessary for
today's visitor to make a detour to Wiveton where a pillar box in the wall proudly
displays the VR cypher of Queen Victoria.)

When the Yellow Caravan passed through Stiffkey's narrow street lined either
side by cobbled walls, there were three public houses: The Red Lion (which

welcomes visitors today) The Victoria and the Townshend Arms. The latter named for the Marquess Townshend of Raynham who owned most of the land in Stiffkey until the 1920s.

Today there is a campsite at Stiffkey—High Sand Creek beside the marshes on the approach to the village from the west—land that was purchased from the Ministry of Defence in the 1970s.

Near Morston we hired a carthorse
To help us up a hill
And again beyond that village
Came another, funnier still.

At Morston they hired a groom and a carthorse to help them get up the hill to Blakeney, this time having been warned there was a steep hill ahead. This is where the road meets the start of the Cromer Ridge, terminal moraine left behind by the Ice Age. The ridge is formed from the sands and coarse flint gravels washed out from the edge of a vast continental ice sheet that reached its southern limit here—which is why there is a sudden change in the landscape.

Morston today has an award-winning hotel and restaurant, Morston Hall; the Anchor Public House in the main street, and Scaldbeck Cottage with B & B and its own campsite for tents with a superb marsh view. From this delightful site it is only a short stroll to Morston Quay where boats leave to take visitors to see the seals. Both grey seals—with pointed nose and white pups born in winter—

going up morston Hill with a hired horse.

Morston hill and view over fields and the marsh to the sea from the top, 2019.

and the smaller common seals, who have round noses and pups born in summer.

While Canham fetched the hireling
I scouted on ahead,
While Judse and Win prepared the tea
And put butter on the bread.

Along there strolled an old man,
A ragged tramp was he,
He stood and gazed for some time
At the interested Sie.
And then he passed the time of day
With those who made the tea.

"These roads are somethin' awful"
He first began to say,
"And only those who have to
Would ever come this way,
They always go by other roads
Who caravan to play".

"I know all about the roads
I'm a travelling man myself"
The others smiled sublimely,
They were sitting on the shelf.

One parting glance at Siezer
And he sloped on his way,
And Canham, and a horse and man
Came on to join the fray.

They hitched the carthorse on in front
The whips began to crack,
The men began to yell, and then,
Nought could have held them back.

Like artillery in wartime
They thundered up that hill;
The pots and pans shook round the van,
I can hear the jingle still!

Siezer bit the strange man
In the leg as he tore by
He kicked her off him as he ran,
I saw her hedge-wards fly,
No harm was done to either
E'en now I can't think why!

We got to Blakeney about 5.30. Only 9 miles but we started late and there were the hills.

We safely got to Blakeney
And then began to hunt
For a mythical "Mr Hudson"
We caught him on the front
By the front, you know, I mean the quay
That at seaport places seems to be.

While Win and Judse were buying bread
Like anyone might be,
An unseen catlike tiger sprang
Upon the peaceful Sie[1].

Its furry arms around her neck,
Sie screamed all round the shop
The baker chased it, loaf in hand
"Cat, cat, come here, Cat Stop!"

A friendly race are those who live
At Blakeney on Sea
And a pretty place they live in too,
At least so thought we three.

Blakeney is a flourishing little town very popular in summer with visitors from all over the country and beyond. It has a busy quay and excellent facilities for recreational sailing and walks along the marsh. The winding high street, with delicatessen, pubs, gift shops and cafés slopes steeply down to the quay. In 1912 the quay was busy with commercial traffic: coal was coming into Blakeney from Newcastle, fish going out to Lynn, grain exported to France and the Low

---

1 *Siezer.*

Blakeny.   Blakeny quay.

Countries as well as being sent to London. The colliers were too large to come into the tidal port, but barges with flatter bottoms went out to meet them and brought the coal to the quayside. The vaulted under-croft of Blakeney Guildhall was used at one time for storing coal—its attractive arches are said to be made from Flemish bricks used as ballast on return voyages from the Low Countries.

The former lifeboat house on Blakeney Point is where the National Trust Coastal Rangers stay whilst caring for Blakeney Point and its wildlife. In 1911,

Unloading a Lynn Coal Boat at Blakeney.

Old lifeboat station, Blakeney, 2009.

when the whole of the Calthorpe Estate was sold, Professor Oliver purchased Blakeney Point. A year later in 1912 he donated it to the National Trust and Blakeney Point became the first nature reserve to be established in Norfolk.

George Hudson had grown up at Manor Farm (now the Manor Hotel) part of Lord Calthorpe's 1000-acre estate—sold in 1911. Mr Hudson was the Harbour Master and coxswain of Blakeney Lifeboat and in 1912 he was still managing Manor Farm and gave his permission for Win, Honor and Judith to park their caravan on the marsh directly in front of the house.

When Judith and Win went to buy bread, poor Seizer got chased by the baker's cat all around the shop. There was only one baker in Blakeney at the time: Mr Charles Russell, baker and corn chandler. Honor wrote:

I then went to forage and got 6 eggs from the post office and some milk and sausages: Sausages, gooseberries and bread and milk for supper tonight. The rain has stopped and it is a fine evening.

They realised they had used all their water after washing up and Charlie Canham had already left for the evening to find a spot for himself and the horse to sleep within the complex of Manor Farm buildings. The girls ventured out with their storm lantern and a bucket to search the farm's extensive buildings and after a few minor adventures they found a water-tub to replenish their supply:

We forgot to ask where dwelt the pump
That night, e'er Canham left,
And by the time we'd washed up
All of water were bereft.

So Judse and I then sallied forth
With bucket and storm lamp,
We tried a marsh stream as we passed
The grass with dew was damp.

The "marsh stream" was a failure,
It was stagnant, smelly and green,
We thought we'd search the buildings,
We could see no other stream.

With storm lamp burning dimly
We left the marshy bog,
We'd rather qualms for fear that we
Should rouse the farmyard dog.

Through an endless maze of buildings,
At last I spied a tank,
But that again was stagnant,
And, to say the least,—it stank!

Then we drew round a corner
And on the midnight air
('Twas really only ten o'clock)
A curious noise we hear,

As if all the goslings in the world
Were hissing at us there,
Then I'm afraid we turned and fled
As if they were hunting us instead.

Our courage soon came back again
And we turned to the chase,
Till at last we thought no water lived
Upon that awful place.

Then in a dingy corner
We spied a tub so fair,
And returned with a bucketful to camp,
Like dogs with tails in air.

DAY FOUR

More Hills to Climb

Saturday 1st June 1912
Blakeney to Kelling Heath (7 miles)
via Salthouse and Weybourne

*We loafed about Blakeney all the morning
and drew a little. The quay was very pretty,
so was High Street and so were the marshes.
We bought some more eggs and sausages to
take on our journey and some bread.*

Blakeney quay.

Next day a boy past o'er our field,
"What's on?" says he to me,
I answered "Nothing's on, we're off"
As we were trying to be.

*After lunch while we were packing a small boy who was going across the field
asked me what was on. I suppose he thought we were a show of sorts. I suggested
nothing was on but we were just off and he left.*

We hitched a horse on either end
To try and turn us round
As we had sunk some inches deep
Into the yielding ground.

The Blakeney Camp.

*We got another horse to help us out of
Blakeney. To turn the van round they
hitched a horse each end and it looked so
funny. We all photographed it.*

Mr Hudson would have helped find a horse and horseman from Manor
Farm to pull the caravan out of the mud. The horse hitched to the back of the

A horse each end to pull us round (Blakeny)

Turning the van round starting from Blakeney.

caravan would have helped to steer it round, being used rather like a rudder, as it would not be pulling in the opposite direction. Only yards from the spot where they were stuck, on the east side of the village is a small area called Friary Hills, now owned by the National Trust. This is near the site of a fourteenth century Carmelite Friary and overlooks the Blakeney Freshes—freshwater grazing marshes. These are fed by underground springs and tributaries of the river Glaven running through a series of sluice gates and flowing into the salt-water of Blakeney Pit and Cley Channel. The Norfolk Coastal Path goes around the perimeter. A little further, just off the coast road between Blakeney and Cley is the unmissable Wiveton Café made famous by the television programme *Normal for Norfolk* featuring its delightfully eccentric owner Desmond McCarthy.

Cley was pretty

Cley-Next-the-Sea—or was in mediaeval times when the Glaven was navigable. Now the sea is three quarters of a mile away, which until 2006 was kept at bay by a massive shingle bank. Evidence of Cley's time as a port still exists with a Customs House (now a private house). Norfolk Customs officers were on the lookout for contraband such as smuggled glazed stone bottles of Dutch Gin. Cley's High Street is narrow and very busy, although in 1912 the Yellow Caravan would not have had a problem negotiating parked cars or oncoming traffic.

Cley Marshes, cared for by Norfolk Wildlife Trust, attract water birds in their thousands giving Cley Marshes an international reputation for bird-watching. In 2007 the Norfolk Wildlife Trust opened an eco-friendly visitor centre on the coast road out of Cley towards Salthouse. The ultimate Norfolk landscape can be appreciated from its long upper floor window. On a clear day it is possible to look out over the fresh water grazing marshes, reed-beds, saltwater marsh and shingle ridge to the sea in a panorama from Cley to Salthouse. Although the coast-line changes over time, and white spoonbills now replace herons, had Honor, Win and Judith pulled in off the road in the same spot and stood on the roof of their

Crossing Cley marshes by beach road, early in the 20th century.

Cley marshes from the visitors' centre, 2019.

Yellow Caravan in 1912 they would have taken in much the same view:

To the left lay all the marshes
And beyond, the salt sea rolled,
And herons rose from pastures bright
With buttercups of gold.

There were a lot of herons on the marshes before Salthouse. Salthouse was a bit bare.

Past Salthouse in its hollow,
Then up an awful hill,
The brake, alas, came quite unswerved
When we wanted to stop still
And rest our gallant panting stead
And the van slipped back again full speed.

Yells came from Canham and from those
Who screwed and screwed in vain,
A stone was placed beneath the wheel,
And all was peace again.

The screwing Honor refers to is the handle on the brake. Having put a stone under the wheel to stop the van slipping backwards, it would have taken the horse quite a bit of effort to get going again on an upward slope. Travelling along the Coast Road, Honor is likely to have found Salthouse *a bit bare*. Fifteen years earlier in 1897 Salthouse had suffered from a great storm. An eye-witness account tells us, *between eight o'clock and noon the crests of the breakers were visible to an unusual extent above the ridge of the sea-wall. Presently a rent was made, speedily to be followed by others, and mighty waves poured inland, filling the dykes and flooding the marshes. To such a height did the water rise that the waves in some cases broke against the upper storeys of the houses, flowed out by the back doors, and destroyed the buildings and garden produce in the rear. Furniture was washed out of houses, fowls were drowned by the hundred and several of the villagers had to be taken out of their bedroom windows by boats and barely escaped with their lives.*[1]

In the East Coast floods of 1953, 30 houses were destroyed in Salthouse and a woman was drowned having been swept out of her house. The surge occurred at night with no prior warning. During a north-westerly gale, when the wind prevents the first tide flowing out, the next high tide comes in over the top of the first one and there is nothing that can be done to stop the subsequent surge. In the tidal surge of December 2013 the sea flooded Salthouse properties, but with today's more accurate weather forecasting people were properly prepared. Salthouse residents were temporarily evacuated to the village hall during the height of that storm.

The Coast Road winds its way gradually uphill from Salthouse towards Kelling, with gorse high on the right and the marshes spread out below on the left. Bright yellow gorse flowers are at their best in late May—although they stay in flower most of the year, hence the saying, *When gorse is out of bloom, kissing is*

Between Salthouse and Kelling, Crankham barn ruin with sea beyond, 2019.

1 Dutt, W., *Highways & Byways in East Anglia*, 1901 reprinted 1904 p. 225

out of season.

At Kelling we hired another horse,
With Kelling Hill in sight;
And then we camped on Weybourne Heath
And entertained that night.

We had come up a pretty bad hill just after Salthouse without any help, but
with several rests on the way. At Kelling we hired a horse to pull us up the hill
to Weybourne. We got to Weybourne at 5.30. On the top of Kelling hill on the
heath we met Almeria Mann and Rose Hamond. Almeria had got our permit
to camp on the heath, but we had to stick close to the road as we couldn't pull
far in.

The additional horse hired in Kelling, with a man to look after it, helped take
the Yellow Caravan to their next camp site on Kelling Heath, as it was an uphill
journey all the way. It is puzzling that Trenny did not provide the Yellow Caravan
with two horses at the beginning of the journey. Unfortunately, it is not a question
we can put to Trenny. It would have saved a lot effort of hiring an additional
horse, with a man, every time there was a hill to be negotiated ahead. On the
flat, a second horse could have simply walked behind the caravan and changed
places occasionally to rest the front horse. Again, Honor and friends had been
previously advised that they would need the assistance of a second horse and
doubtless this was arranged through the Estate Office in Kelling. They turned

right in Weybourne village and then took
the right fork up Holgate Hill. The road
steepens through trees, levels out and
then goes uphill again. On an awkward
corner is a turning to the right (today
before reaching Holt Garden Centre with
Partridge Café on the left). Here there
is an unmarked clearing and space for
parking. This was their campsite.

Obtaining a permit to camp would
not have been difficult for Almeria to
organise. Almeria's uncle, Nicholas
Hamond, a bachelor of 66, was at the time
the Land Agent at Westacre, working for
'HB' (Judith Birkbeck's father) and living
at High House Farm, Westacre. He would
have known exactly how to contact Ernest
Tillett, in Kelling Estate Office to apply

Holgate Hill, 2019.

Left: Mount Zion on Kelling Heath, near Spion Kop, 2019.
Right: View from Honor's Mount Sion over Weybourne to the sea, 2019.

for a camping permit for the Yellow Caravan. Communications were generally by letter or telegram in 1912.

The whole Kelling Estate of about two thousand acres had recently been purchased by Henri Deterding, the founder of Royal Dutch Shell. He had not yet taken up residence there, as he was about to rebuild Kelling Hall, and did not move in until the following year (1913). Succeeding Henri Deterding as the head of Royal Dutch Shell in the 1930s was August (Guus) Kessler who also enjoyed Norfolk country life. He rented Congham House, the Elwes family home, for two consecutive summers for his large family. Raoul Dufy was commissioned to paint the Kessler family on their horses at Congham which they brought with them and stabled there. The striking eight-foot high Dufy portrait is now part of London's Tate Gallery collection.

Honor refers to the hill above their Kelling Heath camp as 'Mount Zion'. On modern maps it is named 'Telegraph Hill' and just to the west on a modern Ordnance Survey is marked 'Spion Kop'. Spion Kop is Afrikaans for 'vantage point' and the name was no doubt attributed to the elevated position by its Dutch owners at the time, the Deterdings. On Telegraph Hill (240 ft. or 73.3 metres above sea level) the trees have been cut back to give a good view over Weybourne and the sea. A short distance away there is an Ordnance Survey Trig Point hidden in an overgrown copse. This takes the form of a stone pillar marked with three angles and is one of Norfolk's 400 Trig Points. Trig Points in different forms were placed mainly on church towers in Norfolk to assist in mapping the country. All are obsolete today on account of GPS, drones and apps.

This was the first party that
We gave upon our trip
And the dinner that was hot and good
Went off without a slip.

Almeria and Rose came to dinner. We had pea soup, stew, cabbages and asparagus, gooseberries, cornflour and cream and lemonade. The dogs barked

lustily at every passer-by. They are awfully good and seem quite comfortable under the van. We had two fires this evening and the guests helped to wash up!

A word here about the clothes the girls wore: in 1912 ladies' skirts were down to the ground—most inconvenient for travelling, clambering up ladders

Judes & Honor cooking sausages

and cooking on a camp fire! The girls appear to wear skirts in dark shades of fabric such as serge or cambric. They wear white or pale shirts, probably cotton or poplin, sometimes with dark coloured ties. The aprons they sometimes wear, tied in a big bow at the back, were possibly also made of poplin. This would have been considered to be normal everyday wear—equivalent today of jeans and a t-shirt. They wore lace up boots well above the ankle and straw hats on their heads. When Blanche Mann came to visit, with her daughter Almeria and niece Rose Hamond, the visitors are wearing more formal clothes with decorative hats. Blanche was a widow, and a former Miss Hamond. The Hamond family (with one 'm') have lived in the north Norfolk district since Tudor times. Blanche appears to be wearing a black two-piece suit, whilst her daughter and niece are in formal, lighter-coloured suits and wearing decorative hats. Rose Hamond never married but continued to live at Weybourne. Almeira married Charles Edward Gordon Hallett (1888–1970) and their son Nick Hallett served with the Royal Norfolk Regiment in the Second World War.

At Weybourne the scenery changes again where the shingle spit of Blakeney Point joins the coast. There is deep water here and to the east the Norfolk Coast Path runs along the top of Weybourne cliffs towards Sheringham. The shingle beach at Weybourne has been described as our Achilles heel since the time of the Armada. The great depth of the water here allows large ships to anchor close to the shore, which in times past was also used by smugglers. In the early 19th century, when Britain was at war with France, the coast at Weybourne was again defended and a warning chain of bonfires were kept ready to be lit all along

Weybourne beach, 2007.

the Cromer Ridge. In the Second World War at Weybourne there were six heavy field guns pointing out to sea. The site of the Military Camp at Weybourne is now the very informative Muckleburgh Collection of tanks, military vehicles and ephemera.

DAY FIVE

Weybourne Church and Priory Ruins

Sunday 2nd June 1912
On Mount Zion with views to Cley church, Cley windmill the marshes and all Salthouse and Kelling.

Next day, being Sunday, we stayed still,
Not sad to have a rest,
Mount Zion's top was peopled o'er,
The view from there being best.

It poured till about 9. So we had breakfast indoors, and didn't cook anything as we had some cold bacon and potted meat. Win and Judse met Almeria and Rose and Mrs Mann and went to church and I minded the van. Canham insisted on washing up for me although I said I was going to, but I didn't want much persuading. We all lunched with Mrs Mann.

Blanche and her daughter Almeria lived at Weybourne House so it was to All Saints church, Weybourne, that Judith and Win accompanied them on Sunday. It stands in the middle of the village with traffic swirling round seemingly from all directions. The interior of the church is rather austere with no east window, but its chequered flint and brick porch reminiscent of a gate-house is worthy of note. The

Canham, washing up.

Weybourne church porch and the Priory ruin, 2019.

attractive ruins in the churchyard were once part of an Augustinian Priory, dependent on the Priory at Westacre. One of the ruined walls of the Priory has a crenelated appearance, created by the former clerestory windows[1]. It is an interesting and evocative place and has an excellent illustrated explanatory noticeboard in the churchyard.

Cley church from across the marshes, early 20ᵗʰ century.

From the top of a hill called Mount Zion I could see Cley church as it stood on a hill, Cley windmill as it stood on the marshes and all Salthouse and Kelling, but not Kelling Sanatorium, I don't know whereabouts that is.

---

1 above eye level 'clear light' windows.

Cley mill and the channel, early 20th century.

A number of little paths all criss-cross and meet on Kelling Heath. It is easy to imagine that point busy with people admiring the view our heroines had. Although today there are some wonderful views from Kelling Heath, these are more restricted than the view Honor describes from Mount Zion as many trees have grown up in 100 years. However, she would not have been able to see the Sanitorium from Mount Zion. The first Sanatorium to have been built was in 1901 and two years later, surrounded by 35 acres, Kelling Hospital was built. Both were for the benefit of patients suffering from tuberculosis (TB) an infectious lung disease, today virtually eradiated. Kelling was chosen as it was considered somewhat remote and that the disease could therefore not spread easily. The pinewoods and being near to the sea were both factors considered to make Kelling a healthy location.

> *The dogs still bark a good deal at passers. When Judse and I were shaking blankets a pony and cart came past that didn't much like the blankets, but we shook harder and they hurried along. I painted a "changing mysotis" (forget-me-not) and started Goff's (Honor's brother Godfrey) letter as we don't have much time when we're really moving. I think we shall probably be rather late tomorrow getting to Overstrand. After tea we did nothing, but just went to the top of Mount Zion to have a look.*

On the opposite side of Holgate Hill to 'Mount Zion', where the Yellow Caravan was parked, is a footpath leading to Kelling Heath Holiday Park. This has been a location for woodland holiday lodges and camping facilities since 1980 in a park extending over 300 acres. The owners emphasise the natural environment and have created woodland walks and cycle trails. Kelling Heath has its own village store and a halt on the 'Poppy Line', the North Norfolk Railway. Starry nights and star gazing are both great features of Kelling Heath hence the necessity of carrying a torch when going to stay there.

With paraffin our fire we lit,
There was a sheet of flame
Full ten foot high—and piercing yells
From Zion's people came;
Perhaps they thought a lusty shout
Would help to put the fire out!

In addition to the hundredweight of coal on board, for cooking inside the van, the girls also had a supply of paraffin—known sometimes as kerosene—for lighting their paraffin lamp—sometimes Honor refers to the *storm lamp* or the *hurricane lamp*. It had a cotton wick and a glass cover that later gets broken. Very inflammable, they use paraffin to help light their camp fire—so it is no wonder the flames leapt so high. They also *paraffin their sticks* in order to be able to cook a meal on the camp fire when the wood was wet.

DAY SIX

The Norfolk Yeomanry Encounter &
The Tame Goose

Monday 3rd June 1912
Kelling to Northrepps (11 miles)
via Sheringham, Beeston Regis, West & East Runton and Cromer

We hired a horse to help us as it was hilly all the way.

They set off with two horses and a second horseman. The additional horse would have been hired from stables in Kelling. This accompanied them all the way to their next campsite at Northrepps as there were a number of hills to negotiate on that part of the journey.

On Monday morn we started off
For Overstrand on Sea,
The rain came down in dripping streams
But not for rain cared we.
By Runton we came round a bend
And there who should we see,
But fully half a squadron of
The Norfolk Yeomanry.
The Officer in charge, of course,
Came to inspect the van and horse.

Just before West Runton we met a detachment of Yeomanry going to a sham fight on Kelling Heath, under Dick and Oliver. Dick came back and had a long conversation.

The Officer in charge was the handsome, debonair Dick Buxton, a Captain in the Norfolk Yeomanry, and with him in the Yeomanry it was Oliver Birkbeck, a cousin of Judith. Dick Buxton knew all three girls well from beagling together with HB's pack of Westacre beagles. Although it was a surprise to the girls, Dick Buxton knew the Yellow Caravan was on its way and he had probably arranged this 'Welcome Party' to greet his young friends.

Dick Buxton, 1911.

The first Norfolk Yeomanry was formed under Field Marshal the Marquess Townshend, who paid for the uniforms of his 'Norfolk Rangers' who paraded in the park at Raynham after the harvest of 1782. This was followed by the formation of various troops within the county. By 1803 there were 22 troops. These were then amalgamated into three regiments: the Eastern, Midland and Western. In 1901 when Lord Leicester was Lord Lieutenant, King Edward VII wished the Regiment to become the King's Own Yeomanry though they had to parade in civilian clothes at Holkham. The following year, they became the King's Own Royal Norfolk Imperial Yeomanry, their uniform selected by the monarch himself. The King then proposed a Regiment of four Squadrons: A, B, C and D. Annual training camps for the Yeomanry were arranged for training purposes with horses stabled in tents. In 1911 and 1912 these camps were held at Northrepps and it was from there that

Norfolk yeomanry at Northrepps, early 20th century.

a detachment of Norfolk Yeomanry met the Yellow Caravan near Beeston Regis Heath.

Beeston Bump and Beacon Hill (known as Roman Camp) and East & West Runton are all part of the Cromer Ridge. West Runton beach is reputedly the best place to study Ice Age ecology in Britain. The cliffs are chalk and flint, the chalk line only exposed at low tide. In 1990 the almost complete remains of a 700,000 year old mammoth were discovered there. Owing to the size of its remains, only a few selected bones of the West Runton mammoth are on display. Some of the mammoth bones are at the museum in Cromer which also has items of local interest to visitors in its Geology Gallery.

We lunched in a shop in Cromer

With the coming of the railways, Cromer became a very popular holiday destination in Victorian times—and remains so today. Cromer with its pier, sandy beach, cliff top gardens and plenty of family-friendly restaurants has always been a much-visited beach side resort and its streets are buzzing with visitors.

We met the van again at the Pelham Burn's house, where the men lunched and we waited a bit.

Major Henry Pelham Burn of the Bengal Army had been born in Calcutta in 1853. In 1912 he was living at Cliff House on the Overstrand Road in

Cliff House, Cromer, 2019.

Cromer—a substantial villa of flint and brick, one of the older houses in the town with crenelated gables and sweeping views out to sea. Henry Pelham Burn had been attracted to Cromer for his family summer holidays on account of his younger brother, the Venerable William Pelham Burn, having been appointed

Archdeacon of Norfolk. Archdeacon Pelham Burn lived at The Chantry, Theatre Street, Norwich, whilst Vicar of St. Peter Mancroft: and he was fortunate enough to have a secondary residence at 36 Church Street, Cromer—conveniently two doors down from Cromer Church (with a tower 160 ft. high— the tallest in the county). A visit to Cromer could include this important building, thankfully much restored by the local Buxton and Cabbell families, even if only to see the Pre-Raphaelite window at the east end of the south aisle designed by Edward Burne-Jones working with William Morris. From Cromer church it is two minutes' walk to the Cliff top mansion where the Archdeacon's brother lived. Contemporaries with Honor, Win and Judith were the two elder daughters of Major Henry Pelham Burn. They were Lucy and Mabel, 24 and 23 who were on holiday at Cliff House.

Cliff House had been owned in 1810 by the Banker Samuel Hoare and later added to with some eccentric Victorian details, particularly its triangular porch of decorative barge boards. Cliff House stands in a commanding position on Cliff Drive. It made the perfect spot for the girls to meet up with the Yellow Caravan again, after lunching in one of Cromer's restaurants. Unlike the narrow streets of Cromer, there was plenty of space for the van to turn around in Major Pelham Burn's driveway. It would have been a joy for Honor, Win and Judith to stand on the bracing cliff top looking out to sea. Charlie Canham would also have appreciated the company of the horseman from Kelling with whom to pass the time of day in the sunshine on top of Cromer Cliffs. The two of them were in no hurry to finish their lunch and get going onwards to Northrepps.

> Then we pulled on again and stopped at Mr Frank Barclays for permission to camp in the Northrepps Woods, which was granted.

Mr Frank Barclay's house was only five minutes'

Burne Jones window, Cromer church, 2019.

Cliff House porch, 2019.

walk along the Overstrand Road from where the Pelham Burns were staying on Cliff Drive. The Warren was a large rambling family house in a wooded cliff-top position. It was originally a pretty Georgian house but much enlarged in Victorian times to accommodate bigger families. Warren Cottages nearby housed coachmen and other staff. The

The Warren, Cromer, in the 1890s.

original house was pulled down and replaced with much 1930's development. Five minutes further on down the Overstrand Road the Yellow Caravan passed The Grove, another attractive Georgian building, now a hotel. The Grove had been the main Barclay family residence in Cromer and is reminiscent of refined Cromer social life 100 years before the visit of the Yellow Caravan. Cromer was a sophisticated resort in the Regency period, at the time Jane Austen was writing. She wrote in her novel *Emma* that Cromer, *is the best of all sea bathing places with very pure air*. At that time The Grove was the summer residence of Joseph Gurney. He not only named it after his Norwich home, The Grove at Lakenham, but planted the impressive wealth of trees along the cliffs behind it as shelter against the North wind.

In Northrepps Wood by Overstrand
We camped amid the trees,
It had taken Judse some time to find
The keeper with the keys.

Two Miss Pelham Burns came to tea. We have a lovely camping place, quite the prettiest we've had. Then Chen came down and Una and later Gladys and Ivy.

The prettiest we have had. The Yellow Caravan was at Northrepps—this is the real thing—today it goes by the name 'Forest Park'. It is one of the few spots where the Yellow Caravan camped that it is possible to do so today and it has wonderful views through the woods and rhododendrons. There are panoramic hilltop views across Cromer Royal Golf Course to the sea. The famous 'Green Walk' as laid out by Repton is a central feature of the hundred acre site. One of the first purpose-made camping sites in Norfolk, which started informally in 1958, Forest Park is still owned and run by the same family.

'Chen' (Richenda Gurney, 23) and Gladys (20) her sister both lived at Northrepps Hall, and were sisters of Quintin Gurney (28, married to Pleasance Ruggles-Brise). Ivy (Ivy Every, 20) was married with a small baby; she and her husband Ted (Sir Edward Every, aged 25) were guests at Northrepps Hall for the duration of the Norfolk Yeomanry Camp there. Ted and Ivy were beagling friends of Honor and Win from Congham. Their names appear in the visitors book at Northrepps for 3rd and 4th June 1912 besides those of Dick Buxton and Primrose Ralli. Ted Every had brought his horse with him to camp, as all members of the Yeomanry did, and he lent it for some of the girls to ride and jump.

Una (Eugenia Barclay, 27) was from Hanworth. Her father, Henry Albert Barclay, was ADC to King George V and commanded the Norfolk Yeomanry. Una often stayed with her cousin Olive Backhouse (24) at Cliff Lane Cottage, Overstrand. Very much part of the social scene, Una Barclay was once again staying there, her visit coinciding with the Norfolk Yeomanry annual camp at Northrepps. Her future husband—

Forest Park camping site, Northrepps woods, 2019.

Gerald T. Bullard of the Bullard brewing family—was also a distinguished member of the Norfolk Yeomanry. The previous summer, Captain Gerald T. Bullard had commanded the detachment of Norfolk Yeomanry at the Coronation Parade for King George V on 22nd June 1911. Together with his future father-in-law, Colonel Barclay, they were both awarded Coronation Medals.

Ivy jumping. Gladys Gurney

Mrs Zigamala has again written to Win this time for what to take in the van. She is going in August.

Mrs Zigamala, had married a businessman from Manchester, who was half Turkish and half Greek. Hilda Zigamala was planning to take the Yellow Caravan on a holiday along the North Norfolk coast with her teenage son and his friends later that same summer.

We shall probably stay here

2 nights and then to Honing in one day. We shall probably have a lot of entertaining to do! During supper, which we had in the van because of the wet, Vera Kerr and her sister came to call so we invited them to breakfast at 8.00 tomorrow.

**That evening after supper
We were visited by two,
Whose tame goose waddled with them
As no other goose would do.
But it got into our water pot,
Which it enjoyed but we did not.**

Yellow Caravan can be seen at the far end of the avenue

Honor confused me at first with the spelling of Vera's surname. But it seems she is referring to Vera Carr, then aged 21, daughter of the Rector of Overstrand, the Reverend Lawrence Carr and his wife Olive. Vera's little sister Violet was only 14 at the time and was being educated at home at the Rectory by her governess, Miss Maywood. The tame goose lived at Overstrand Rectory on Paul's Lane and likely belonged to little Violet. I am told that geese, when tamed, are great companions if you keep eye contact with the gander first, crouch down and talk softly and never hiss back if the goose should hiss. It was just a short walk up a steep path from Overstrand to where the Yellow Caravan was parked in the beautiful woods at Northrepps. The Carr sisters were accompanied by the goose the first evening, when it insisted in getting into their galvanised water container, but they left the Rectory Goose at home when they came as guests to breakfast the following morning.

DAY SEVEN

Black Shuck and The Slippery Cliffs

Tuesday 4ᵗʰ June 1912
A second night in Northrepps Wood and a visit to Overstrand

It was fine till after breakfast. I jibbed at getting up at 6, but we got up at 6.30. The guests arrived to breakfast without the tame goose, who came with them last night and would drink our drinking water! We parafined our sticks well so were able to cook all right.

Chen came to elevenses of Bovril and Biscuits.

Guests all next day came trooping down
But in the evening, we
Went down to shop in Overstrand,
And walk beside the sea.

Judse and I went down to Overstrand and got some bread and a chop for Canham's dinner tomorrow.

The village of Overstrand was never reached by the railway and therefore stayed more refined and exclusive than Cromer. A number of large villas can be seen on the cliff top, including The Pleasaunce where some buildings were designed by Lutyens, with a garden originally laid out by Gertrude Jeckyll.

Dick rode down and had a look at us while were lunching.

Dick Buxton, who had met the Yellow Caravan the previous day when the Yeomanry were on their way to the sham training fight, was taking part in the annual Norfolk Yeomanry camp in the park at Northrepps. Dick was taking great interest in the goings-on of the campers and keeping an eye out for his young friends.

Peggy came down in the morning too. After lunch Ivy, Gladys and Vera Kerr [sic] rode past and I put up the jump for them which they got over all right.

Peggy, Una Barclay's younger sister, was the same age as Judith Birkbeck (25). Ivy's husband, Ted Every, had lent his horse for Vera Carr to ride that afternoon. Members of the Norfolk Yeomanry all brought their own horses with them to Camp. Later, in 1914, when Lord Roberts put out a call for horses and saddles

Vera Carr, jumping on Ted Every's horse. Northrepps.

for the British Army, the Norfolk Yeomanry were reluctant to part with their own animals for anyone else but themselves to ride. But in the event, the Norfolk Yeomanry became mounted on bicycles. They obviously had a deep affection for their horses which they somewhat naturally found impossible to transfer to their bicycles.

Win and I were fools enough
Upon the cliff to play,
It wasn't like a common cliff
And when we'd got half way
We slipt, we fell, could scarcely move
Up to our knees in clay,
So thought we'd climb that silly cliff
Upon some other day.

Win and I went down the village and onto the beach by a steep path she knew down the cliffs. Then she paddled and Kai played round. He'd never been down on the shore before and couldn't think why the sea was salt! Then we thought we would climb the cliffs by another route . We got ever so high after frantic struggles because there were lots of little streams and all round them were positive quagmires! Eventually after getting a plant or two we came to the conclusion we couldn't get up that way, so came down. It was clay and greasy. My foot slipped and I slid about three yards. I was filthy!.

From the cliff top there is a steep path down to Overstrand beach. Overstrand Cliffs are another of Norfolk's sites of Special Scientific Interest. The cliffs occur at the end of the 'Cromer Ridge' and from the beach—which is a good place for fossil hunting after a storm—can be seen the soft creamy chalk with angled lines of flint running through. After much rain, as in the summer of 1912, the cliffs would be very soft and slippery.

Overstrand beach and cliffs, 2019.

We eventually got safely down and up the way we'd come and bought some eggs and hurried back to the yellow van by 5.30 and found Judse had made a cornflour pudding for the Honing dinner party tomorrow night. We had tea and hustled her off to the camp as she wanted to see Harry play polo.

Judith's eldest brother (Major) Harry Birkbeck was also at the Norfolk Yeomanry Camp at Northrepps which would have created some quite sociable occasions—a polo match being one of them.

We stayed and painted. Win did a quick sketch of the rhododendrons which are lovely and I painted my Buckhorn Plantain and Cutleaved Saxifrage and Maratima Campion and started the dumplings to go into the soup tonight.

The soup is the water the chicken was boiled in at lunch which they like to call
chicken broth! However, on eating it I found it absolutely delicious and took
back all the things I said against it at lunch time!

Judse and Win went forth to look
At the moon across the sea
And came tearing back a little late
As frightened as could be.

They'd talked so long of ghosts and spooks
Their minds were in a fog
Till coming home they thought they saw
Old Shock, the headless dog!

Now Shock's a dog without a head
Who is supposed to trot
Along the roads round Overstrand,
Once seen, is ne'er forgot.
But Shock's been seen by very few,
And chiefly by the folk who knew.

There are many folk tales about Black Shuck and a number of different
names for the ghostly animal that was supposed to roam along the coast between
Beeston and Overstrand. Honor is likely to have used Dutt's *Highways & Byways*
as a guidebook, and may even have based her Black Shuck verse on a traditional
ditty: *A dreadful thing from the cliff did spring, And its wild bark thrilled around, His*
eyes had the glow of fires below, 'Twas the form of the Spectre Hound.

W. A. Dutt, in his 1901 *Highways & Byways in East Anglia*, describes the
creature thus: *He takes the form of a huge black dog, and prowls along dark lanes and*
lonesome field footpaths, where, although his howling makes the hearer's blood run
cold, his footfalls make no sound. You may know him at once, should you see him, by
his fiery eye; he has but one, and that, like the Cyclops', is in the middle of his head.
But such an encounter might bring you the worst of luck: it is even said that to meet
him is to be warned that your death will occur before the end of the year. So you will
do well to shut your eyes if you hear him howling; shut them even if you are uncertain
whether it is the dog fiend or the voice of the wind you hear.

DAY EIGHT

A Comfortable Bed for the Night

Wednesday 5th June 1912
Northrepps to Honing (11 miles)
via Thorpe Market, Antingham, North Walsham
and White Horse Common

Got up early and were away by 9. Quintin lent us a horse to pull us out of the wood and as far as the North Walsham Road. It poured and sluiced and deluged till about 11.30, then we had no more.

Next day as we passed Antingham
We nearly killed poor Kai,
Who cut his leg against the wheel,
And sent yells to the sky.

But he walked on all right again,
And then we to North Walsham came,
We met two short steep bits, going down,
So galloped into Walsham town.

I usually go and pick up information when we come to a village and got out to do so at Antingham. I called Kai who got knocked on the wheel but no bones were broken.

Honor stopped at Antingham to look for printed information, but maybe she was too busy attending to her poor wounded Kaiser-dog to realise they had missed the opportunity of seeing the stained glass window in the south chancel of Antingham Church. The three panels were designed by Pre-Raphaelite artists Dante Gabriel Rosetti, Edward Burne Jones and William Morris himself and are an uncommon sight for Norfolk. The window was installed by the Rev. John Dolphin in memory of his mother Martha Dolphin who died in 1864 aged 81. These depict: Saint Martha on the right holding her cooking utensils in her bare arms, designed by Rosetti; in the centre is the Virgin Mary with Easter Lily designed by Burne Jones. The panel on the left, designed by William Morris, features Saint Mary Magdalene—with her very long head of hair and holding a bottle of aromatherapy oil.

> *We were just past the North Walsham flour mills, when a motor appeared and out hopped Zil Duff—a person known to me by name and personally by Judse.*

By Zil Duff, Honor is likely to be referring to Catherine Duff from Westwick—just three miles away. Catherine's brother had changed his surname to Petre when he inherited the Westwick estate—on which there is a plantation named 'Duffs'. Their father, James Duff, had been MP for North Norfolk. Catherine, 35, was ten years older than Judith, and may have been driving the car herself—Honor is not clear on this point. The name 'Zil' confused me as I thought it had to be short for Basil. But when I discovered Catherine's second name was Basilia I realised it was a good fit. Their meeting place was Ebridge Mill on the Dilham Canal. The former flour mill is an attractive industrial building of red brick with a slate roof which has today been converted into apartments. From the mill, the road runs uphill to Honing Hall.

> **Later we got to Honing Hall,**
> **Our blankets steamed with wet**
> **When they hung them by the kitchen fire,**
> **So awfully damp things get.**

This window is unique in the county containing the only glass designed by the renowned Pre-Raphaelite artist Dante Gabriel Rosetti, 2009.

Ebridge mill, 2019.

When we got to Honing the coachman at the Cubitt's bathed him (Kai) for me and put some stuff on, so I hope he won't be very stiff tomorrow.

Judse has a bit of a headache so went to rest as soon as she got to Honing. We camped in the Park near the house and had tea there and I believe some are coming out to dine, but am not sure so will add later. Anyway, we're all sleeping in (the house) tonight. Aunt Ysabel is going to stay there and arrives soon and must pass the van to get to the front door!!

Honing Hall, 2019.

The coachman at the Cubitt's was George Brown, who lived with his wife Ada in the coachman's cottage, attached to one wing of the stable block behind the house. Mr Brown, who looked after the horses and carriages at Honing, and therefore used to looking after animals, would have been the person tending to Kaiser's wounded leg. In the kitchen at Honing, where Miss Martha Brown reigned supreme as the cook, it seems to have been a surprise to Honor that their blankets from the caravan *steamed with wet* when hung in front of the kitchen range. Jessie Bean, the housemaid who had come from Little Snoring, or Gladys Palmer the under-housemaid, a Lowestoft girl, would no doubt have had to ask permission of Miss Brown, the cook, if they could hang the blankets there for the night. Doubtless the butler, cook, kitchen maid and footman were likely to have lighter duties that evening, as Mrs Cubitt and her 26 year-old daughter Christel were being entertained to dinner in the Yellow Caravan. Arrangements would have to have been made below stairs, however, for Charlie Canham and the Westacre coachman to have their supper. Ysabel Birkbeck may have also been accompanied on that occasion by Edith Goymer, her lady's maid. The Westacre coachman probably had driven them over by car from Westacre to coincide with the visit of the Yellow Caravan. In 1912 the footman at Honing was Launcelot

Honing Staff in the 1890s with Mr & Mrs Edward Cubitt.

Horner. However, at one stage prior to the First World War, there was a Chinese footman at Honing called Mr Ho. Footmen had various tasks which included answering the door, polishing the silver, laying the table and serving at breakfast as well as general errands. One of Mr Ho's duties was to fetch the fresh fish in a hamper off the Yarmouth train at Honing Station and drive it to the Hall by pony and trap. The excitable Mr Ho was once caught trying to send the Honing cook to heaven with a carving knife, mistakenly thinking that was what she would have wished!

Whether there was a little parental disapproval of the Yellow Caravan can only be guessed at, but Honor's exclamation marks following her note that Aunt Ysabel *…must pass the van to get to the front door!!* is suggestive of possible minor disapproval by the older generation to the caravan expedition.

So after they'd all been to dine
They took us back to sleep,
And we left the old van by itself,
The dogs the watch to keep.

(Added later) They came to dinner! Aunt Ysabel, Mrs Cubitt and Christel and we had such fun and such a dinner: Mock Turtle soup, chops, vegetables, stewed apples and cold cornflour and cherry jam. The vegetables consisted of asparagus, cabbage and potatoes and were all cooked in the same caldron owing to a shortage of saucepans! Then we washed up, left the dogs in charge of the van and slept indoors. It was so funny arriving at a house I'd never been to before with my toothbrush in my pocket and sponge and nightgown under my arm!

DAY NINE

A Brush with the Law

Thursday 6th June 1912
Honing to Horning (12 miles)
via Dilham, Smallburgh and Neatishead

Confusion sometimes arises over the similarity of the names of these two villages: 'Honing' means 'The People on the Hill', and 'Horning' means 'The People on the Bend', or the Horn, the big bend of the River Bure.

We left about 9.30 with Mrs Cubitt and Aunt Ysabel on each shaft to see what it was like. But they only went to the next drive gate, but Christel on a bike came as far as Smallburgh to see us up the hill. In Honing village we stopped and greased the lock of the van.

Christel Cubitt & Judith at Honing.

Honing forge today, 2019.

83

We left that cheery household then,
And started on our way again,
It was a most exciting day
And scarcely raining, strange to say.

Oiling the lock—this photograph was probably taken by Christel Cubitt on Honor's Box Brownie camera. It is outside Mr William Bunting's blacksmith's shop in Honing village. The same forge is still in evidence today at the top of the village street. The lock on the Yellow Caravan consisted of two metal disks about three feet across, pivoting one above another: one for the caravan and one for the fore-carriage. There were no bearings. The lock would need to be greased occasionally. The grease is in a tin on the ground. The man working on the far right is wearing hobnail boots and an apron. He is greasing the gap between the two turntables and the man at the front has a long-handled brush which he is using to prise the two turntables apart. They would then move to the other side of the caravan and prise apart the second side and repeat the exercise.

Today driving down Honing Long Lane in the Spring is a delight—a mile of white daffodils sweep across the verges on either side of the road. It is a memorable sight, and Honing's 'Daffodil Day' in springtime spreads its fame. Christel Cubitt rode her bicycle beside the Yellow Caravan as far as 'The Crown' in Smallburgh. After Smallburgh, the next village the girls head for is Neatishead. Following the 1912 Ordnance Survey, the road runs in almost a direct line from Honing to Horning.

The mounting block, seen on the right in the previous photographs, has moved but a few feet since 1912, 2019.

After Christel left, we were all walking along in front of the van and never heard a rubber tired dog cart come and if the trusty Canham hadn't yelled "Mind" we should certainly all have been killed!

Between Neatishead and Horning came a dog-cart. This was not a vehicle drawn by a dog (such carts were prohibited in Britain in the early 1900s on animal welfare grounds). Honor is referring to a light horse-drawn two-wheeled vehicle, sometimes known as a 'bounder' originally designed for transporting dogs. A box behind the driver's seat had room for one or more retrievers or other sporting dogs. The 'dog box' could also be converted to a second seat to accommodate a passenger.

I don't like Neatishead; we stopped for lunch about a quarter of a mile from the village and drew the van off on one side of the road and made a fire on the other and cooked our lunch of poached eggs and sausages. A horse and cart drove past and shied and reared so it nearly upset. The men went to the village and sent the policeman after us to move us on. He was half in plain clothes and having got no change out of Canham came to see us. But we insisted on finishing our meal and I personally laughed so I nearly choked—the others had hysterics without that! Then we moved!

When Neatishead we had passed
We stopped to have our lunch at last.
We took the horse out, lit the fire,
And who'd have thought 'twould raise the ire
Of passers-by in carts, although

The horses past us scarce would go!

We raised the wrath of one, whose horse
Objected to us, and of course
Kaiser and Sie set to to bark
What said he as he passed us? Hark!
That surely wasn't meant for us
'Twas stupid of the horse to fuss.

But yes, he meant what he had said,
And a policeman came from
Neatishead,
"Are you the gentleman" said he
"Of this concern" and readily
Canham answered him instead
"Are you the Constable?" he said.

Canham brought him round to us
Lunching in the van,
The man he took a look at us
And we looked at the man.

"Ladies" he said "You must move on"
"And I must see you go"
At that I had a choking fit
For I was laughing so.

You're committing great offence" and we
Saw he was getting vexed
"Canham, first we'll finish lunch"
Was what we gasped out next.

And finish it indeed we did
Before we made a start
And he was thankful when he saw
The van and us depart.
We'd no respect for arms of law
Whom we had never seen before.

Police Constable Herbert Locke had been only been in post at Neatishead since October 1911 from where he was also responsible for Irstead and Barton Turf. It is not possible to confirm if it was indeed PC Locke who attended the incident on the Neatishead-Horning road on 6th June 1912. If he was away from his beat on leave, another officer could have been allocated to the incident. He may have come on a bicycle, as since 1900 bicycles for village constables were commonplace. PC Locke had come from Ditchingham but did not remain at Neatishead long, as he moved on with his wife and family of four to Horsham St. Faiths in May 1914. At the time, this was not unusual practice as officers were frequently transferred to reduce familiarity with the local population.

Policing in Norfolk in 1912 consisted of many parts. At that time there was a county-wide force of Norfolk Rural Police with twelve or more divisions throughout Norfolk as well as the Borough Police Forces of Norwich, Thetford, Yarmouth and Lynn. Their pay-scales were diverse and many wore different uniforms. (This may account for Honor's remark that *he was half in plain clothes*). The chief constable of Norwich City Police and a number of his officers were mounted. Often their horses were the same ones that pulled the fire-engines— all housed in the same buildings. Gradually the different police forces were amalgamated and in 1968 became known as the Norfolk Joint Police Authority, and in 1974 the Norfolk Constabulary was created.

The girls left Honing at 9.30. Their lunch break, pulling the caravan off to one side of the road and building a campfire on the other then cooking lunch would involve at least an hour and a half, probably two. Added to that was the incident with the Constabulary. This is likely to have taken place where the verge is wide on either side of the road somewhere near the site of RAF Neatishead. Just round the corner is the early warning system controlled by RAF Boulmer in Northumberland as well as the RAF Air Defence Radar Museum. Here a secret radar system was installed during the Second World War to carry out ground-controlled interceptions. The Museum, which it is possible to visit, has 25 exhibition rooms including World War II and Cold War Rooms. Gallery, Crumbs café and shop—all have seasonal opening times.

We got to Horning at 3.

Now Horning, where we stopped that night
Is on the Broads, so we
Soon hired a boat and got afloat,
As happy as could be.

Our heroines' first sight of the broads at Horning coming in from Neatishead would have been magnificent—a little downhill and the river spreads out in front. The view would be equally magnificent today if there weren't quite so many pleasure craft making it hard to focus on the far bank when standing on Horning Staithe by the Swan public house.

Mr Body where Christo told us to camp was out but expected every minute, so we left Canham to get the camp ready and went and got our letters.

A Thatched House on Ropes Hill, 2019.

Mr George Frederick Boddy was the farmer at Ropes Hill Farm, very convenient on the approach to Horning from Neatishead. Ropes Hill Barn is easy to spot at the junction with the Ludham to Wroxham road. On the opposite side of the road, with a little imagination and without its porch, The Croft could have been Mr Boddy's farmhouse.

Horning Post Office at the time was a charming little white painted thatched building on Lower Street, run by Mrs Cox who also kept a shop on the premises. In 1912 letters arrived there twice a day from Norwich at 7.25 a.m. and 3.20 p.m. and were dispatched at 11.40 a.m. and 6.45 p.m. on weekdays and on Sundays at 10.30 a.m. In addition to the Post Office in Horning there was a wall letterbox on the Half Moon Public House on Upper Street. The Half Moon no longer exists, and the Post Office has moved next door to another thatched two-storey building with a Dutch gable and interesting chevron brick-work. Its wall letterbox is new Elizabethan. The proprietors of

A Wurry on the broads Horning.

Horning Post Office are as friendly today as no doubt Mrs Cox was when the young ladies of the Yellow Caravan called to collect their letters, sent 'Poste Restante' to await the girls' arrival.

We went on the Broads, or rather the river, for a two hour row. It was lovely. I got my first sight of the Broads and a wherry.

The Broads were formed from flooded mediaeval peat diggings. When peat was dug, sea and river levels were lower than today. Originally the Broads were quite shallow, but from the beginning of the 20th century, they were dredged. In 1909 the river Bure at Horning was a mere 3'3" deep and in those days Horning Village Street was lined with boat building sheds. The river 'traffic' before holiday makers arrived consisted of the traditional wherry, with its tar-coated black sail, used for transporting grain, coal and other goods up and down the rivers. Norfolk reeds harvested and tied into long bundles for thatching were carried by traditional flat-bottomed lighters. A lighter had no sail but was propelled by a 'quant' a long pole reaching down into the mud that also acted as a rudder for steering.

The Norfolk Broads became a holiday destination after 1907 when Harry Blake came with friends from London on holiday on the wherry *Olive* owned by Ernest Collins. Harry Blake then started advertising Broads Holidays to would-be visitors. By 1909 Blakes were acting for more than a dozen boatyards and other yachting businesses followed. Horse-drawn coaches also brought fishing parties to stay in Horning from Norwich and Yarmouth.

A thunderstorm came on after tea and it was very wet. So we cooked our mackerel inside. We bought some from an old man in a cart in Horning. I got some flowers today: Wild Camomile, Prickly Lettuce and Corn Ranunculus.

The fish Honor purchased off the cart would have been quite fresh, but not caught in Horning! Mackerel would be caught in the sea at Great Yarmouth, and brought to Horning by wherry.

DAY TEN

Drama on the Ferry and a Picnic Dinner Party

Friday 7th June 1912
Horning to Postwick (7 miles)
via Woodbastwick and Little & Great Plumstead

We went on the Broads again this morning in a sailing boat for two hours. It was lovely.

Next morn we took a sailing boat
E'er we went on our way,
We liked it so we almost wished
We could prolong our stay.

Judith & Honor in a row boat on Horning Broads

Judith in the sailing boat at Horning, looking worse than she felt

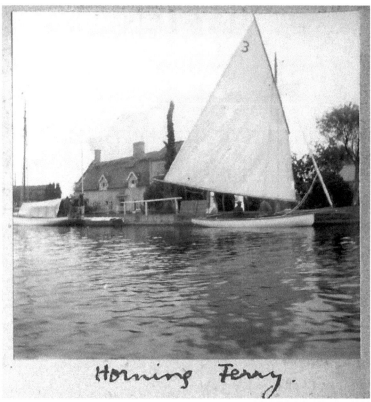

Horning Ferry.

St. Benet's Abbey early 20th century.

Horning Ferry Inn.

We can just see the tip of the boom of their sailing boat at the very left of the picture. Beyond that are the white railings of Horning Ferry.

The best way to get a sight of the Broads is from the water itself. By renting a day boat from Horning, which is what Honor and friends were to do, there are a number of places to visit. The important ones are St. Benets Abbey (an hour and a quarter by water from Horning, remembering that the speed limit is 4-5 mph on the Broads) and Ranworth (three quarters of an hour by water from Horning). It is possible to visit both on the same day.

St. Benets Abbey: on the way to St. Benets you will pass St. Benedict's Church at Horning with its own Staithe. The rector of Horning also holds the title, Prior of St. Benet's Abbey. St. Benet's, further down the Bure River, also has its own landing stage. St. Benets Abbey stood on an island, Cowholm, and was endowed by King Canute 1000 years ago. Little remains except for the gatehouse into which was built a mill in the eighteenth century. Painted in 1808 by John Sell Cotman, it became one of his most famous paintings and is widely reproduced. Standing on firm ground surrounded by the marshes, a modern crucifix has been erected on the site where the high altar once stood. The Bishop of Norwich remains to this day the Abbot of St. Benets and he arrives by boat for an annual traditional Sunday service in August which is a unique and memorable sight.

Ranworth on Malthouse Broad—so named for the quay having been used for unloading barley for malting—is the home of the Norfolk Wildlife Trust centre and is thatched with local reed. This floats on a pontoon at the edge of the

Broad. It is half a mile from Ranworth Staithe and reached by a boardwalk. Alternatively, there is a ten-minute ferry service from the Staithe to the Wildlife Centre which is full of fascinating information about the Broads, and has wonderful views from it across the water. When visiting Ranworth, make time to look in St. Helen's church, sometimes described as the 'Cathedral of the

The Horning foot ferry, 2019.

Broads'. Not only does Ranworth have an exceptional mediaeval rood screen taking up the whole width of the church but a magnificent illustrated mediaeval missal of 285 pages of sheepskin vellum. A climb to the top of the church tower gives energetic visitors the most wonderful Broadland view.

But we left in the afternoon,
And came to Horning Ferry soon.

In 1912 the proprietor of the Ferry Inn, advertised as *central for the Broads and good accommodation for visitors*, was William Crowe who also described himself as a "Wherry Proprietor". Mr Crowe ran a family business at the Ferry Inn with help of his wife and two of his five daughters. His 16 year old son Walter was an apprentice boat builder. Also living at the Ferry Inn, at the time, was ferryman Arthur Middleburgh, aged 20, who had come from Sprowston. The passenger ferry service ran from the Ferry Inn and was used by locals to cross the River Bure to Woodbastwick with horses, carts and cattle and for the Horning baker, Mr Sims, to deliver his bread to Woodbastwick and Ranworth. Horning Ferry was a chain ferry resembling a floating pontoon—with posts and rails round the sides and was propelled across the river by a chain cranked by a shaft.

A Second World War tragedy occurred in April 1941 when German bombers hit both the Ferry and the Ferry Inn with much loss of life.

Today there is a foot ferry operating in the summer months. The ferry boat takes passengers and bicycles across the river from Horning to Woodbastwick: otherwise road travel is 8 miles round via Wroxham Bridge or 18 miles by Ludham, Potter Heigham and Acle bridges.

We left Horning at 2.30 and went first through Horning village, over Horning Ferry. Horning Ferry was the first excite! The horse fell on its knees getting off and Siezer flew out of the door like a catapult stone! But neither were the least hurt and we went on through the usual pouring rain.

The Ferry would sink down a bit when the front wheels got on, so that the van was at an awkward angle. The wooden deck of the ferry would also be slippery when it was wet, and we know from Honor it was constantly raining. It is possible that the deck of the ferry may have had wooden slats across the centre so that wagon horses could get some sort of grip—in the same way as a modern horsebox has slats up the slope.

The Brick Kilns, Little Plumstead, 2019.

The Ferry sank when all got on
A good six inches drop,
And Canham grasped the horse's head
"We'll do it quite all right" he said
"We've not yet had to stop".
The horse slipped down, got up, then took
The whole thing at a run,
And Sie was sitting on the shelf,
Just looking out for fun,
But at the six inch jump, you know,
She flew like arrow from a bow!

The lamp glass missed the lemonade
As it sprang to the floor,
It also missed two chickens fat
That we had cooked before,
For that eve at Postwick, wet or fine
Another party came to dine.

At Little Plumstead we stopped and had tea in "The Brick Kilns" and a very good tea it was too.

A visit to a public house would have been an unusual experience for the young women—but Honor simply reports the facts. The Brick Kilns was a very convenient stopping place then, as it is today. The public house was named after the brickworks at Little Plumstead, just five minutes' walk. Gunton Brothers' brickworks produced ornamental brick mouldings there before the First World War. Guntons' 1908 catalogue lists whole ten-foot high ornamental moulded and crenelated brick chimneys for little over £3 each. They also supplied the ornamental bricks for The Grand and

Gervase Birkbeck.

the Metropole Hotels in Cromer (neither still stand) as well as for the Royal Hotel in Norwich. The Little Plumstead brick yards closed in 1939.

> *We have another dinner party tonight so bought some more little soup bowls in Little Plum before we left. Well before we got to Postwick village we camped in Mr Water's meadow, (as arranged by Christo).*

Judith had two more brothers (besides Harry who was playing polo at the Northrepps Yeomanry Camp). The others were Gervase (28) and Christo (23). They motored over to dinner at Postwick that evening on a pre-arranged plan. Christo had organised for our heroines to camp that night in a meadow belonging to Charles Waters, farmer and grazier at The Grange. Christo was working at Sprowston at the time as a land agent with Michael Falcon in Falcon & Birkbeck. Michael Falcon had come to Norfolk to be the land agent at Blickling for the Lothian family. He came from a long line of Michael Falcons in Cumbria which had been their home since 17th Century. It was Michael Falcon's son (also Michael) who captained the Norfolk Cricket team from 1912 to 1946. A colossus in Norfolk cricket, he scored more than 11,000 runs and took over 700 wickets by the time he retired in 1947. Another great Norfolk cricketer was Christo Birkbeck's brother Gervase. The previous season, Gervase had scored 672 for the County including two not-out innings of 89 and 75 against Suffolk. A quiet and unassuming man, he worked in Barclays Bank in Kings Lynn. On Friday 7th June 1912 he had probably left work early and had driven in his car via his home at Westacre to pick up a fresh Westacre trout, and then on to Sprowston to collect his brother Christo. Sprowston to Postwick is only 5 miles—so very handy for this Friday evening dinner party. Honor was particularly fond of Gervase who,

like his older brother Harry, was in the Norfolk Yeomanry. Besides the trout, the brothers had brought with them a Fuller box of chocolates and some *picture papers* which may refer to *The Strand Magazine, The Sketch* or *Illustrated London News.*

> *We had soup with dumplings in and cold boiled chicken and fried potatoes, stewed lettuces and hot cornflour pudding with jam underneath—such a feast! But it was so wet we didn't wash up but left the things till tomorrow.*

That night again, to say the least,
We sat down to another feast
Soup and Dumps, potatoes fried
And fowls, and lettuce stewed were tried
And Judse a cornflour pudding made
And the drink we had was lemonade.

"The Party" left a Fuller box,
Some papers and a trout,
Judse cooked the fish next day when we
Had time to look about.
'Twas so well done, 'tis strange to tell,
No cook had cooked it half so well.

Postwick today is not famed for its long grassy meadows, summer evening *rendez-vous* or charming picnic spots. Today Postwick has a large Park & Ride facility for convenient travel into Norwich. It is on the A47 Southern Bypass, a road that cuts Postwick in half. Mr Waters' Grange, Grange Cottage where his coachman lived, and the picnic meadow are all on the north side of the A47. Postwick village itself is charmingly tucked away on the south side of the bypass. In 1912 the plan for the following day was to head south down Ferry Lane and to cross the next river—the River Yare.

DAY ELEVEN

Ferry Across the Yare and into South Norfolk

Saturday 8ᵗʰ June 1912
From Postwick to Dunston Common via Surlingham Ferry, Bramerton,
Framingham Pigot, Framingham Earl and Stoke Holy Cross (8 miles)

A ferry here was first recorded in 1665 by a reference to 'New Ferry Way' at Postwick and in 1682 it was reported that a seal had been shot in the river near Surlingham Ferry. During the early 18ᵗʰ century the Ferry House at Surlingham was the property of a Lady Barbara Ward. By 1908 the Brewers had the ferry rights and when the Yellow Caravan made the crossing in 1912 Steward & Patterson were the brewery for the Ferry Inn, Surlingham, and Henry Rawston the publican. Henry Rawston's son Thomas was the ferryman. However, as Honor mentions *the old ferryman* in her diary of the day, it was more likely that Henry Rawston himself was in charge on that particular day. The ferry in those days was operated by hand, and winched across the river on a chain in the same way as the Horning to Woodbastwick Ferry.

We couldn't light our fire next morn,
It never ceased to pour;
Win warmed our water on the lamp,
While we gasped by the door
That storm lamp smoked and smelt as it
Had never done before.

Surlingham Ferry was most exciting, the horse was nervous and having got the van just on refused to pull it into the middle, so it had to be unharnessed. The old ferryman was very frightened but we got over all right. Horning Ferry only cost 9d. but this cost two shillings.

99

We crossed a ferry at Surlingham,
The horse was rather scared,
'Twas so wet we were well pleased
when
Stoke Holy Cross appeared.

Crossing the Yare was quicker in the old days—just over 50 yards (48m) from bank to bank. To drive from one side to the other today it would be necessary to go 10 miles round by the A47 and Trowse. However, for anyone wishing to have the chain ferry experience of crossing the Yare as Honor and her friends did 100 years ago, it would be possible to motor 10 miles from Postwick to Reedham on the north side of the river Yare and cross Reedham Ferry. The Ferry Inn at Reedham has camping facilities and the chain ferry takes three cars at a time. To pick up the route of the Yellow Caravan, it would then be necessary to drive 14 miles back towards Surlingham on the south side of the Yare. From Surlingham it is easy to follow the old ferry route through leafy lanes with high banks on either side— signs of an ancient track. The roof of the Yellow Caravan would be touching the trees that arch over the narrow lanes

Looking across Yare to Surlingham from Postwick. The Ferry House on the other side, 2019.

Norwich/Surlingham ferry sign, 2019

Leaving Surlingham Ferry for Framingham Earl, 2019.

creating tunnels of dappled green, sunlight barely reaching through—but on the 1912 journey we know it was raining most of the way! Ferry Road, Surlingham, leads into Bramerton Road and becomes Surlingham Lane, Bramerton. There is then a choice of three different lanes the Yellow Caravan may have taken to cross the main Norwich to Loddon road. Sallow Lane, Fox Lane and The Street, Framingham Pigot are all delightful and reminiscent of Norfolk 100 years ago. It is worth driving round in a small circle to appreciate all of them, before coming out on Pigot Lane, near to the building of the East Anglian Children's Hospice at the Railway Tavern on the Norwich to Bungay main road.

Once more it was wet till about 3. It was so wet we postponed the washing up and got them done in the "Railway Tavern" at Framingham Earl.

Railway Tavern, Framingham Earl, 2019.

The Railway Tavern at Framingham Earl was so named around 1845 expecting to be near a planned station on the Norwich to Halesworth line. Owing to lack of funds however, this line was never constructed. A later proposal in 1896 linking Norwich with Beccles also failed on account of its high cost of £96,000. Instead, an omnibus service was introduced in 1905—but the name Railway Tavern remained. Today, the Railway Tavern at Framingham Earl is as friendly and as accommodating as it was in 1912 and, when asked the question, replied they would be happy to assist a group of passing travellers in distress unable to wash up their crockery!

> *Judse walked up to Poringland to see if Mrs Birkbeck was at home but she was away but she found out that Geoffrey Birkbeck was at home, so we went on there and arrived at 2 or thereabouts. It was nice there and how they laughed at the van. The rain stopped and we looked round the garden which was so nice.*

The Yellow Caravan went on to Upgate, Poringland, from where Judith walked up to 'Poringland House', later known as 'The White House' and *pleasantly situated on the southern slope of Poringland Hills* (Kellys Directory of Norfolk 1908). Having established that Mrs Ethelreda Birkbeck was not at home, the girls travelled on to Stoke Holy Cross, having learnt that Mrs Birkbeck's artist son Geoffrey was at home at Stoke Hall. Stoke Hall no longer exists, although a half-timbered

The White House Poringland. In 1912 it was known as Poringland House, the home of Mrs Ethelreda Birkbeck, Judith's great aunt, 2019.

Stoke Hall, c1915.

Victorian lodge to it, designed by Salvin, is easily identified on the left-hand side of the road leading towards Stoke Holy Cross church.

Lodge to the former Stoke Hall, 2019.

As the rain had stopped, our heroines were invited to look round the beautiful gardens of Stoke Hall which were often the subject of Geoffrey Birkbeck's paintings. There were acres of beautiful gardens at Stoke, described at the time as, *decorative as any in Norfolk and laid out with singular charm and beauty, luxuriant with woodland and ornamental trees. On the south side of the house was a wide terrace walk lined with shaped yew bushes, an oval sunk garden with ornamental pond and fountain and a small formal garden of herbaceous beds with yew and cypress hedges and a shady lime walk.*[1] Geoffrey Birkbeck also planted a long avenue of trees across the park towards Stoke Holy Cross church, visible from the house. Stoke Hall had been designed by Salvin for the Birkbeck family in 1852—a red brick mansion of 28 bedrooms with 63 bells to answer in the butler's pantry. It became the home of Geoffrey & Dora Birkbeck on the death of his father—Geoffrey's older half-brother Henry Birkbeck, 'HB', having moved to Westacre High House.

> **They gave us lunch and tea and then**
> **Set us on our way again,**

---

1 *Poringland Archive*

We were troubled buying bread,
No baker lived in Stoke 'twas said..

When Judith, Honor and Win left Stoke after their garden visit,

They started us off with heaps of kindling and tried driving in the van to the village. There we stopped at the shop and bought a lamp glass, ours having broken crossing Horning Ferry, and several other things and the dogs frightened one child and we frightened the little girls in the shop—one quite solemnly backed out of the shop and we heard the little one telling her mother "Some big womans with a van was inside and they frightened me". Then as there was no baker in the place we bought a loaf at another pub and went on to our destination, Dunston Common.

The little incident at the village shop where their presence *frightened* two little girls is an indication that strangers did not often visit Stoke, and the children felt uneasy at the sight of people with whom they were unfamiliar. The shop, however, was well stocked enough to supply a replacement glass cover for *Former village shop, Stoke Holy Cross, 2019.* their paraffin lamp. The shop was likely to have belonged to Mr Herbert Clarke situated on the right-hand side of the road coming back towards the village from Stoke Hall. A very picturesque white-washed double fronted house with sash windows, sitting within its own pretty picket fence, just one door down from Stoke Long Lane is no longer a shop, but a private house. Unsurprisingly, today there is still no baker in Stoke. However, the young ladies were able to purchase a loaf of bread from a pub. There were two pubs in Stoke in 1912, the 'Red Lion' (now an excellent gastro-pub 'The Wildebeest') and a little further on 'The Rummer Inn' which today is a private house, but fortunately the eight-foot high post for the Rummer's inn sign is still visible on the grass verge. The unusual name of the inn is for a glass drinking vessel with glass studs in the stem. It is probable the Yellow Caravan visited the 'Red Lion' for the loaf of bread being nearer the turning they next took into Mill Road. There they passed the spectacular Stoke Mill, situated on its narrow bridge over the River Tas (today Stoke Mill is a restaurant serving lunches and dinners). It was at this mill in the mid-18th century that Jeremiah Colman started his mustard business which became such an important industry for Norfolk. The mill bridge over the River Tas is so narrow that only one vehicle can pass at a time—and for the Yellow Caravan on its way to Dunston Common it may have been rather a tight squeeze!

Stoke Mill where Jeremiah Colman started his mustard business, 2019.

We arrived at Dunston Common at twenty minutes to six and had to wait till the Agent came home before we properly camped, as no one was allowed to without his leave! He arrived soon after 8 but we'd given up waiting and had started cooking our supper. He knows Christo and he didn't mind us camping.

On Dunston Common we encamped
Though leave we had to ask
From the agent, but as he was out
We really couldn't wait about,
So each set to our task.

Win stoked the fire, I scrubbed the van
And Judse some dinner cooked
And when the agent passed, he laughed,
And said it really looked
As though we meant to camp and so
'Twas no good telling us to go.

On Dunston Common time stands still, although today it would not be possible to camp there. The caravan only pulled a short distance off the road and into a delightful spot—more or less where today's visitors are invited to park their cars. Beyond is an inviting clearing in the wood and a modern children's play area with a little wooden house and climbing frame, with a public footpath leading into the dark unknown. To the north-west, the row of houses where the land agent, John Beck, lived is now known as Stoke Lane, but in 1912 it was part of Dunston Common. There is no tarmac here—it is an old fashioned dusty track—a seemingly identical surface to that which the Yellow Caravan passed over. The houses along the lane today look much the same as they would have done in 1912—the Common Dairy Farm and Common Farm. It is a tranquil

Dunston Common, 2019.

and attractive spot and standing there it is easy to imagine the atmosphere of a Norfolk lane of 100 years ago.

It is hardly surprising John Beck did not arrive at Dunston Common until 8.00 in the evening to see the young ladies. He was a busy man: he looked after 600 acres at Dunston, 1,660 at Stoke and 1,500 at Shotesham. John Beck was a bachelor of 23. He had been educated at Greshams School and had gone on to learn his farming and land agency at the Aspatria Agricultural College in Cumberland[2].

Large country houses built by the Victorians were becoming something of a burden to their owners and conversions to country house hotels had not really begun. In 1912 Dunston Hall which had been built and owned by the Longe family, was let. The tenant was Geoffrey Fowell-Buxton, a banker in Norwich with a large family—all away from home when the Yellow Caravan was camped on Dunston Common. He kept a large indoor staff of twelve, a coachman and four grooms. Aside from his banking interests, Geoffrey Fowell-Buxton had purchased in 1897 a pack of hounds from Colonel Unthank of Intwood which became known as the Dunston Harriers. The Dunston Harriers covered the same territory in South Norfolk as the Norwich Staghounds, with whom Sir Alfred Munnings later hunted. The Master of both that pack and of the Dunston Harriers for a period was Miss Sybil Harker, a descendant of the family of J & P Coats thread-makers of Paisley. Munnings was to paint Miss Harker riding side-saddle, a picture that was sold in 1990 for over a million dollars. Dunston Hall was built in 1859 on the site of a much earlier house and stayed in the Longe family until 1957 when it became a furniture store for Wallace Kings. It was converted into a hotel in 1993. Beyond the Common, on the corner of the main Norwich to Ipswich road, looking towards Dunston Hall, is the site of the former village cricket pitch, long since incorporated into Dunston Hall golf course.

---

2 *This college closed in 1914 at the start of hostilities and never re-opened. Cirencester Agricultural College, on the other hand, closed in 1914 but re-opened in 1922.*

Stoke Hall, Stoke Holy Cross by Geoffrey Birkbeck with Theodora & Billy Birkbeck on the terrace, 1911.

DAY TWELVE

Geoffrey Birkbeck, Norfolk's Leading Watercolourist

Sunday 9th June 1912
A second night on Dunston Common, church at Swainsthorpe and a visit to Stoke Hall

Judse and Win went down to get the milk. Mr Beck wouldn't hear of them paying their two pence. He's also sent us down a loaf of home-made brown bread.

The milk was doubtless from the Common Dairy Farm at the end of Dunston Common—the likely residence of John Beck.

He sent a loaf of home-made bread,
For us to eat next day,
He gave us all the milk we wished,
Helped us look out our way,
And let us hire a horse and man
That Monday, that could draw the van.

Sunday it was so off we went
To Church a mile away,
At Swainsthorpe, where we got in late
As we had lost our way.
Some small boys were in front, who made
Grimaces at us while we prayed.

Dunston Common Dairy Farm, 2019.

We went to Swainsthorpe Church this morning. We had some difficulty finding our way as we got wrong in Dunston Park. (All the Dunston people are away from home). We arrived late and sat at the back. There was a row of small boys in front, who amused us hugely. One turned round and made such a face at me. I should think he was about four. I grinned, so he did and we ended quite friendly. The next boy and he got their noses almost touching and then sang loudly "As it was in the beginning". It was awfully funny.

Today, St Peter's Church at Swainsthorpe is easy to find off the main Ipswich Road, standing at the top of Church Road. It is one of Norfolk's round tower churches, probably pre-Norman. On the wall of the south chancel is a brass plate remembering Captain Gilbert Havers who served in Queen Elizabeth I's army in Berwick on Tweed, Scotland, Ireland and the Netherlands and died in 1628 aged 87. It is not possible to sit where Honor did at the back of the church, as St. Peter's is a church without pews, and has a large space for functions and a kitchen.

Swainsthorpe Church, 2019.

Mr Beck came up after lunch and we looked up our tomorrow's journey; we're hiring a trace horse from him. We want to get to Hingham and next day near Swaffham and Wednesday end up at North Wootton.

On Sunday afternoon John Beck promised them a trace horse and a horseman for the following morning to pull the Yellow Caravan as far as Hingham. Living at Dunston Hall stables were the coachman and four grooms, the eldest of whom was Sydney Wick aged 29. However, it is likely that John Beck asked his neighbour Lawson Mann aged 50, who was described at the time as the "Horseman on the Farm", to accompany Charlie Canham and the young ladies on Monday morning. In the photograph of the group when they reach Hingham, it appears that Charlie Canham is talking to an older man, which discounts any of the Dunston grooms, beside it being convenient on a Sunday afternoon to ask his neighbour to accompany the little party. It may perhaps have been Mrs Mann who baked the loaf of bread for the girls.

A tea party came down from Stoke
Who loved the yellow van,
Who climbed up on the roof and played
And washed up cup and can.
Who thought it all an awful joke,
And took us back to dine at Stoke.

Geoffrey and Dora Birkbeck and Theodora and Billy drove down to tea. Billy is five and Theodora is eight next Tuesday. They are so funny. After tea Billy and Theodora helped to wash up and I gave her the honey spoon to suck and they all laughed because her face got sticky and she wiped it up with the old string dishcloth. We lit the hurricane lamp for them to swing about and took them on the roof and eventually let Billy down through the skylight. Then as Mrs Birkbeck said she'd like to walk home I got a lift back in the pony cart and we all stayed to supper.

Stoke Party - at Dunstan Common.

Mr. G. Birkbeck.

Geoffrey Birbeck, date unknown.

Around 1912, at the time the Yellow Caravan visited Stoke, Geoffrey Birkbeck painted a picture of his children Billy and Theodora on the terrace at Stoke Hall.[1] The whereabouts of the original is unknown but on account of the sad story that followed, the artist is likely to have had the original of the painting destroyed.

Geoffrey Birkbeck was Norfolk's leading water-colour artist of the era. He was famed for his Norfolk landscapes and had also painted a great deal abroad, in Venice and at Versailles under the early influence of an Italian artist, Onorato Carlandi. Geoffrey Birkbeck exhibited all over Europe and his work was extremely well received in Paris, in London, as well as at the Castle Museum in Norwich. Geoffrey Birkbeck was received into the Roman Catholic Church in 1901 before marrying in 1904 his first wife Dora. From the personal reminiscences of Father Raphael, a friend of the artist, we learn that Geoffrey Birkbeck saw less of his extended family except for those who were Roman Catholic and one of them was Aubrey Buxton whom he taught to paint. The artistic Geoffrey wore floppy bow ties as a mark of his Bohemianism, kept Dalmations for their decorative effect and spoke in a high-pitched squeaky voice. Father Raphael also recounts that Geoffrey Birkbeck installed in the chapel at Stoke Hall the altar and baldichino (canopy of state) from the chapel of the Venetian Embassy in London.

Geoffrey Birkbeck's personal story was a tragic one. Sadly, his wife Dora and their beloved daughter Theodora both died of typhoid from having eaten oysters somewhere in London. Theodora died in December 1924 aged 19 and her mother only eight weeks later in February 1925. After these shocks and his utter despair, an admirer of his work, Mrs Hore-Ruthven, who lived in Bracondale Woods, wished to help him recover from these great sorrows. She suggested he occupied himself and paint murals of Venice on the walls of the big dining room of her house.[2]

The Birkbeck family graves in the churchyard of Stoke Holy Cross, 2019.

1 page 106.

2 These murals no longer exist as Bracondale House was pulled down in the 1960s to make room for County Hall.

Stoke Hall's former wooded position from Stoke Holy Cross churchyard, 2019.

Five years after the death of his first wife, whilst on honeymoon in Europe with his second wife Maud Barrett, Geoffrey Birkbeck received the news from Stoke that his son Billy, aged 23, had killed himself. Geoffrey Birkbeck sold Stoke Hall and it was pulled down in 1938. Stoke's wooded former position can be seen across the fields from the churchyard of Stoke Holy Cross, which itself stands on a promontory with views across the lovely Tas Valley. Geoffrey Birkbeck, who died in 1954 having married for a third time following the death of Maud, is buried at Stoke Holy Cross. The family all lie in a secluded spot in the churchyard near a stone pillared pergola, under which hangs a carved wooden figure of Christ crucified. The churchyard faces the site of their former home—a most evocative place. The White House, Poringland, to where Geoffrey had moved after leaving Stoke, had become, during his time there, the Sunday Mass centre for Roman Catholics in the immediate district. After Geoffrey Birkbeck's death, and that of his third wife Daisy, the White House later became the property of the Roman Catholic Diocese of East Anglia.

> 'Twas dark beneath some shady trees
> When we were going back,
> When a huge great black dog padded by
> That never even winked an eye
> Or wandered from the track,
> But like some ghostly shadow, he
> Ran on swift and silently.

Canham & the horse
at Bradnham.

DAY THIRTEEN

The Longest Day

Monday 10th June 1912
Dunston to West Bradenham (24 miles)
via Mulbarton, East Carleton, Ketteringham, Wymondham, Crownthorpe,
Wicklewood, Hackford, Hingham, Woodrising, Cranworth, Letton Hall,
Shipdham, East Bradenham

A colossal day! Our longest journey, 24 miles.

Next day we got to Bradenham,
The longest day we'd done,
We didn't reach our camp until
The going down of the sun.

We hired the Dunston Estate horse from Mr Beck with a man, to go to Hingham.
It was a lovely horse and pulled the whole van and let ours go behind. Canham
rode it, and I think found it a little painful, as it had to jog the 15 miles to keep
up. We bought a bit of food in Wymondham, sausages for breakfast and stuff
for Irish Stew.

The original plan, as outlined by Honor the previous day, had been to get to
Hingham. It is unlikely that they left before 9.00 in the morning which appears to
be the usual format of the day. Honor tells us in her diary that on this particular
day Canham was riding their horse behind the caravan and he had to jog to
keep up. Pulling the caravan was the trace horse from Dunston—a seemingly
stronger looking horse. The girls could be riding in the Yellow Caravan with
Lawson Mann, the Dunston horseman, driving the horse, rather than leading
it. From Dunston to Wymondham they made good time. The road was relatively
flat, but tree-lined, rural and even today has little traffic. From East Carleton
to Wymondham the road runs past the Ketteringham woods. Eight miles into
their journey, the party stopped in Wymondham to shop, which could have been

accomplished in an hour from Dunston at trotting pace.

Wymondham is another of Norfolk's delightful market towns: it has a charming central Market Cross, octagonal and half-timbered. No doubt they parked the Yellow Caravan near to it. There are shops in Wymondham today where you can buy *sausages and stuff for Irish Stew* and anything you might need for your picnic.

Wymondham Abbey, 2014.

The jewel in Wymondham's crown is its Abbey—a beautiful symbol of Norfolk's heritage. The mediaeval monks who first came to Norfolk always chose picturesque spots for their abbeys and monasteries and all stand in attractive surroundings. Wymondham Abbey's two towers (one for the Monastery and one for the town) can be seen in the landscape for miles around.

> *We lunched at a farm called Crown Thorpe about one and a half miles through Wymondham. It rained heavily for about half an hour but that was the only wet all day. I made some dear little dumps to put in the stew.*

Crownthorpe was a small village of 35 houses in 1912 when there were two farmers, Herbert Wade and Joseph Holah. The latter, with an ancient English surname meaning 'Hollow', had come from a farming family in the Fens. In 1912 the farms at Crownthorpe were part of the Kimberley Estate[1]. Honor mentions stopping at *a farm called Crown Thorpe*, a farm which today is known as Whitehall Farm. But Whitehall Farm is at the top of a long drive and away from the direct route in which the Yellow Caravan was heading. It is more likely that the party pulled in at Wood Farm, Crownthorpe which is close to the road and easy to pull in to eat their lunch of Norfolk Dumplings and Irish Stew. Wood Farm is situated on the more direct route through to Wicklewood, Hackford and Hingham. It could have been that Honor had asked for the name of the place where they parked for their lunch, and the answer came back *Crown Thorpe*.

(In 1958 the remaining 4,000 acres of the Kimberley Estate were sold, including Kimberley Hall, and a number of tenants purchased their own farms, as the tenants of Wood Farm and Whitehall Farm were able to do. Today there are three farmhouses in Crownthorpe and five houses including the church, which is now a private dwelling.)

When we had got to Hingham
'Twas twelve on our way,

---

1 *Kimberley in the 1880s had once consisted of over 10,000 acres.*

And we sent back the horse that we
Had hired for half a day.

Canham, who had jogged behind
On our horse, all the way,
Said he hoped he wouldn't suffer so
As he had done that day.
The horse we'd hired was fine and fat
So there wasn't any chance of that.

At Hingham we sent back Mr Beck's man and horse and put our own in and
went on to Shipdham.

Hingham with no cars and no urban clutter: you can see its midday by the size of the shadows. In Honor's photograph we see her with her back to us: over her left shoulder is Charlie Canham. He rode the horse from Dunston to Hingham when the Dunston trace horse was pulling the caravan. He found it uncomfortable as cart-horses were not meant to be ridden and their harness did not include stirrups or saddles. Canham would have been sitting on the back pad of the harness.

The Dunston horseman, who we believe to be Lawson Mann, is looking into his money bag. The Dunston horse, that will shortly be returning home, is on the right of the picture. On the left we have someone new—elegant and well dressed: she is Mrs Mason from Necton. I consulted Jenny Lubbock and Richard Blake to ask what their great-grandmother was doing in Hingham, 12 miles from where she lived, Swaffham being her obvious shopping town.

Changing horses at Hingham.

Mrs Mason's brother was the Rev. Arthur Upcher, Rural Dean and Rector of Hingham at the time. Hingham Rectory was just a stone's throw from that delightful townscape in which we see the caravan parked.

The Rev. Canon Upcher was obviously much loved. In Hingham's magnificent church there are beautiful kneelers—and amongst them is one in memory of Canon Upcher. The panel of Rector's names was also given in his memory. Sadly, the Rector was to lose a son in the First War along with 800 officers and men in a catastrophic accidental explosion on board H. M. S. Vanguard. It is all there, recorded in Hingham church. In 1912 the Rector of Hingham could walk from the west door of St Andrew's church, down the yew lined path and with a couple of strides cross the Attleborough Road. Straight in front is the Rectory (now a modern replacement) entered through magnificent wrought iron gates.

We met the Mason's just outside Hingham and they said we must call in tomorrow.

It seems that the Yellow Caravan made good time to Hingham and instead of stopping there, as previously planned, having bade farewell to Lawson Mann and the Dunston horse, the party decided to continue on to Shipdham, another six miles.

We'd hoped to camp at Shipdham,
But they wouldn't have us there
And 'twas four miles more to Bradenham,
We were well-nigh in despair,

We tried to camp at Shipdham, but Shipdham wouldn't have us!

Honor is referring to Letton Hall, just a mile and a half short of Shipdham. Letton Hall, designed by Sir John Soane, originally belonged to the family of the First Lord Cranworth. He was Liberal MP for mid-Norfolk and the first Chairman of Norfolk County Council. Following his death before the First World War, his son sold Letton and moved to Grundisburgh in Suffolk. So,

Letton Hall, 2019.

when Honor and Win asked if they could camp there, it is doubtful whether any of the Cranworth family were at home. And therefore, on they had to go.

So into the Golden Dog went we
And had a huge and well-earned tea.

The Golden Dog, Shipdham, 2019.

Doubtless William Ashby—the innkeeper of the 'Golden Dog' in 1912—would have been surprised by a visit of three tired and hungry young ladies. This is the third public house they visited on their trip round Norfolk. (The fourth if we count 'The Red Lion' in Stoke for a loaf of bread). Today the 'Golden Dog' in Shipdham serves lunches at the Bar as well as evening meals.

We wandered on to Bradenham. In West Bradenham lived Canham's brother-in-law who was delighted to put us on a meadow in his little farm.

Canham had some friends who lived
At Bradenham and said
"I know they'll let you have a field,
And the horse and me a bed".

So on we went till seven past
Another four miles more,
When we arrived in camp we'd been
Three miles and a score!

The meadow where we camped was lush
The sunset gold and red
The supper that we quickly cooked
Was soup and dumps and bread.
The dogs were quite as hungry as we
And about as tired as they could be.

Corner Cottage West End, West Bradenham, 2019.

The Coe family living at West End, West Bradenham, were Charlie Canham's wife's family. Living with them was Charlie Canham's great uncle George Canham, who was 95 at the time of the visit. The whole family would have been delighted to welcome him, and no doubt had had some kind of prior warning that he might indeed turn up bringing the three young ladies. The lush field facing west, from where they could see the sunset, is likely to be just beyond the present West Brook Farm. The Coe family and the Canham family once lived next door to one another. At the end of West End Lane, past Westbrook Holidays, where the lane forks left to Ivy Todd is a striking double fronted colour-washed house with a central chimney that could once have been two cottages. Beyond this, just short of the Ivy Todd, boundary, stands another somewhat dilapidated cottage half-hidden by overgrown bushes—a rare sight today. Maybe one or the other of these was once 'Canham's Cottage'.

DAY FOURTEEN

A Steam Roller on the Home Straight

Tuesday 11th June 1912
West Bradenham to East Walton (15 miles)
via Necton, Swaffham and Narborough

Next day, the last that we should spend
With our old yellow van,
I don't know who was sorriest,
Us or the dogs or man,
The horse I know was thankful when

He trod again the streets of Lynn.
We saw more friends at Necton,
And at Petygards we had
A drink, as it was very hot,
And the roads were rather bad.

We stopped some time at Necton, calling and they came and inspected the van.

Necton Hall was once a large Tudor country house of pale pink brick, standing in its own park. It had been enlarged and crenelated in the Victorian period but sadly no longer exists, having been demolished in 1949. Honor, Win and Judith had met in Hingham the previous day Mrs Mason, who invited them to call at Necton on their way past. The Mason family had lived at Necton since the early seventeenth century until Miss Elizabeth Mason died unmarried in 1878. Necton then passed to her second cousin, Robert Blake-Humfrey. On inheriting Necton, he and his wife Jane relinquished the name 'Blake' and added 'Mason'. Living there in 1912 were Mr and Mrs Robert Mason, their daughters Hilda (30) and Audrey (25) and their son Humfrey (27). Just a month prior to the visit of the Yellow Caravan in April 1912, Necton had been the scene of much rejoicing when an elder daughter, Lettice Mason (33), married Guy Lubbock.

Necton Hall, early 20th century.

Their son, Joe Lubbock, who died in 2019 aged 103, told me he had often visited his grandmother Mrs Mason at Necton Hall. He had so loved every inch of Necton that it was a traumatic moment when, years later out hunting, he suddenly realised he was galloping across the foundations of the old house just visible in the grasses.

In the 1912 photograph taken outside the gates of Necton it looks a hot day. I found the curved spot where the front gates of that great house once stood, marked on the map as 'The Follies'. Re-visiting in 2019, with professional photographer Ben Elwes and his camera, who should appear in the very spot but a member of

Curved spot in Necton where the gates of Necton Hall once stood, 2019.

Norfolk's Horse-Driving Club leading a beautiful carthorse cob called Bengy. Nearby, in Necton churchyard, where the Mason family have lain buried since 1617, is an interesting mediaeval stone coffin of a pilgrim. It is said to mark the grave of the Countess of Warwick, who died at Necton on her way to Walsingham.

Bengy the carthorse, 2019.

Dick and his motor met us there. He caught us up after he'd inspected pheasants just after we'd passed some stones and a steam roller.

Having returned home from his stay at Northrepps, the attentive Dick Buxton met The Yellow Caravan again at Necton. This time he was not on his horse but driving his car. It seems he took a keen interest in the route of the Yellow Caravan, as this is third occasion on which he pops up in the story. The girls obviously did not need much persuading by Dick to stop next at his

The lime avenue to Petygards camping site, 2019.

home for a cold drink, a mere two miles on from Necton. Dick lived at Petygards, with his sister Alice and their widowed mother, known to all as 'Aunt Minna'. Petygards (the name means Little Garden) is technically in the village of Sporle but stands in a secluded position. All three young ladies on the Yellow Caravan trip were familiar with Petygards and had been to stay with 'Aunt Minna' on previous occasions. Petygards is a private house surrounded by its own park with an impressive avenue of lime trees leading to it. It has some beautiful specimen trees, Corsican pines and sequoias and several 500-year old English oaks. Today it is possible to camp at Petygards, where the proprietor's Shetland ponies and chickens run freely in the surrounding paddocks.

Honor notes that *the roads were rather bad*, but that was not the only time the subject of the roads had been mentioned during the journey. The travelling man they met near Morston had told them, *these roads are somethin' awful.*

**A steam roller was trying to roll
A long thick strip of stones,
The old horse gazed at it and then
Staggered on with groans,**

And couldn't do it, so we said
"Hitch the roller on, instead!"

But the eight men who were working
Came and joined the fight,
They pulled and pushed their level best
The foreman shouted with the rest
"We don't want them here all night!"

A rush, a yell, and we were o'er,
Those awful stones were passed,
A mile or so and we were then
In Swaffham Town at last.

Road repairs were the responsibility of the parish councils up until the late 19th century. In Norfolk, flints were the only locally available raw material and these came from stone pits or were.picked from cultivated fields by hand. In 1912 the road surfaces were adequate for horse-drawn wagons and were constructed from flints flattened by a steam roller. The long thick strip of stones Honor mentions in the poem could refer to the road being of two narrow bands that were surfaced either side of a central grass strip. George Cushing in his memoirs recalls mending the roads when the by-roads were only nine foot wide. The skilled road-menders seemed to George Cushing to have mystic powers and could plumb a straight line ignoring the twists and turns of the landscape and made measurements like qualified surveyors. Road-menders worked in teams, carrying and spreading the flints from the stack at the side of the road. This was then bound with gravel and chalk like a mortar, which worked well for horses and carts, but the rubber tyres of a car would tear up the road surface and chalk dust flew everywhere. In March 1912 Swaffham Rural District authorised the carting of stone from North Pickenham pit to Necton at 3/6d. per yard and chalk at 2/3d: stone carted from Shipdham Pit to West Bradenham was authorised at 3/8d. a yard. The steam roller Honor, Win and Judith encountered was possibly a Burrell, supplied to a contractor working for Swaffham District Council. Although tarmac had been patented ten years previously, it was unlikely to have been widely used on Norfolk roads before 1930. However, a surveyor's report for Swaffham Urban District Council in September 1911 suggested retaining the necessary tar required for the forthcoming winter, when estimates were produced for steam rolling at £1/4s/6d per day.

Norfolk is fortunate to have the country's finest collection of steam engines and steam rollers at Thursford, near Fakenham, collected by the late George Cushing (1904-2003) who had loved steam engines and fairground machinery ever since he had been a small boy. He set up in business buying a 1913 Aveling and Porter from Walsingham District Council for £225. George Cushing's business prospered and he built up a fleet of 15 steam rollers and a steam wagon. But by the end of the 1930s steam was being replaced by the internal combustion engine, and the old engines were redundant. To George Cushing, it was *as though the crown jewels were being sold for scrap*, and he began to buy up old engines, storing and restoring them and thereby founding the Thursford Collection, turning what began as his hobby into one of the world's most important steam and fairground museums.

By the time the Yellow Caravan reached Swaffham, the trio were back on familiar territory. The Hamond family, from whom all three young ladies were descended, had once owned property in Swaffham including the Manor House. In the seventeenth century Nicholas Hamond had purchased the manor of Swaffham, and unfortunately two of his three sons predeceased him. Probably on account of this sadness, Nicholas Hamond endowed the original Hamond's Grammar School, which moved to 'The Old School House' facing the Market Place. Its 1736 plaque once read, *Nicholas Hamond gave by will in 1724 £1000, 500 for erecting a School House 500 for endowing the same for instructing XX (20) boys in Reading, Writing and Arithmetic. Benefactors who promote knowledge, virtue and industry deserve to be recorded on earth and rewarded in Heaven.*

The Old School House, Swaffham, 2015.

The Butter Cross, Swaffham, 2015.

The Old School House is an attractive red brick Georgian building adjoining another, somewhat earlier and larger, and both buildings appear to be lacking care and attention. Directly opposite these lovely buildings, standing next to the town sign in the Market Place, is a brand new electric pod point for charging electric cars. The town sign features John Chapman the Swaffham Pedlar who, according to folklore, dreamt that he should go to London to seek his fortune. On his return home he found a pot of gold buried in his own garden with which he helped rebuild Swaffham Church. His image, and that of his dog, is carved on the front pew-end of the parish church of St. Peter and St. Paul in Swaffham.

The most striking building on the Market Place is the domed and pillared Buttercross built in 1783 by Lord Walpole, Earl of Orford (whose sister married Anthony Hamond of Westacre). Behind the rotunda is Swaffham Assembly Rooms, built ten years previously.

We went to a chemist in Swaffham to get a bit of dirt out of my eye that I'd got in yesterday afternoon. He got me up into a corner of a window and with a brush and stick got it out.

I hailed a chemist as I had
Something in my eye
He got a little stick and brush,
And said he'd have a try.

He put me in a corner,
Where I couldn't move about,
He used both stick and paintbrush
And at last he got it out.

In 1912 there were two chemists in the Market Place in Swaffham: one was Frederick Christopherson and the other Frederick Cooper. Mr Christophersons' shop had the added advantage of having Bradley's artificial teeth manufacturer in attendance on Friday mornings. Mr Cooper FSMC advertised as a chemist and an optician, so it is more likely Honor was squeezed into the corner of his dispensary. Had her affliction been more serious, there was the Victoria Cottage Hospital on the Sporle Road, established in 1888, today an NHS Community Hospital.

We bought some sausages which we waited for while the man made, and we lunched on them and eggs about a mile from Swaffham. The eggs had to be scrambled as Judse dropped them in the road and broke them as they wouldn't fry. A poor tramp and his wife came by on their way to Wisbech and she asked for some bread which Judse gave her and which pleased her painfully.

Canham + Judith washing up at Swaffham.

There were six butchers in Swaffham in 1912, but only two

in the Market Place where it was likely they purchased the sausages: Edward Rawson was one and Eastman's was the other. Yet another of the Swaffham butchers listed was Walter Smith, farmer and butcher at Little Friars Thorn on the Lynn Road.

Swaffham today has in its Market Place, a barber, butcher, Boots Chemist, café, charity shop, estate agent, florist, newsagent, pizza parlour and pubs. Swaffham has an indoor market on a Friday and a wonderful outdoor market on a Saturday selling meat, vegetables, bric a brac, and plants. The Saturday market has a great atmosphere and is a real attraction for local people and tourists.

> *Through Narborough we got on the roof and lay flat so as not to be seen which I think was pretty successful except that Kaiser jumped onto the van to look for me just after he'd been in a pond.*

As through Narborough we went
Upon the roof lay we
Kai, who'd just been in a pond,
Jumped in to look for me.

Narborough Hall, surrounded by 265 acres at the time, was the home of Mr Joseph Critchley Martin JP, his wife Constance, and daughter Edith (32). For some reason, Honor and company did not wish to be seen as they went past Narborough Hall. With its pale pink brick and crenelated parapet Narborough Hall, built by the Spelman family in its parkland setting in the eighteenth century, was once a delightful sight from the main road. But the Yellow Caravaners did not wish to look! Sadly, a more recently planted hedge now obscures one of Norfolk's finer views.

Narborough village, on the river Nar, once had its own railway station from where, among many other goods, the watercress from Westacre was dispatched to London. Today the disused railway embankment is under the care of Norfolk Wildlife Trust. Narborough Church is well worth a visit on account of the many splendid memorials to the Spelman family. One of them, Clement Spelman (who died in1679) objected to the idea of being walked on and directed that he should be entombed in a stone pedestal in an upright position. And so he remains!

The young ladies' original proposal had been to take the Yellow Caravan back to North Wootton, but it appears their plans were changed. They had already been away from home for two weeks and were en-route for East Walton—from there, they returned to Westacre. It would certainly have been quicker, and more direct, to have turned right in Narborough (and not taken the route past Narborough Hall) and gone direct to Westacre that night. But it was not until they got to East Walton they received a message, likely from the older generation, that the luggage cart was to collect them the following day, and Charlie Canham was to return the horse and van to Trenny's stables.

> We got to Walton and we are being fetched tomorrow and Canham is taking the van home to Wootton. We camped on the field next to Walton Common on Mr Knight's farm. He came round in the evening and took Judse and me round the house. The Beauchamps (see Postscript) have left and he's going into it and it is being repaired and the gardens being improved. He also gave us some radishes for our last night's feast.

At Walton, 'neath a giant ash,
We camped for the last time,
So end the trip and we had had
A simply glorious time.
And as it's over, I must end
This somewhat lengthy rhyme.

> We had a huge fire and had green pea soup and dumplings and fried potatoes and radishes and bread and jam and cocoa. Miss Crawford came over and saw us. After we washed up we went down to the common and had a look and also had a dance round the fire and made weird noises as we had been told to do!

East Walton had few houses, but Abbey Farm and the Rectory are the two big houses in the village. Both are private houses standing next door to each other behind high walls. The story goes that the high wall round Abbey Farm was built to protect King Edward VII from prying eyes when he visited Abbey Farm as a shooting guest of 'HB'—Judith's father. In 1912 HB's pack of beagle hounds were kennelled at Abbey Farm and Mr Knights looked after them there.

Miss Crawford, who came to visit the girls, was the daughter of the Rector. It would have been easy for her to spot both the Yellow Caravan and the campfire from the Rectory. Mr Bill Lewis who today lives at Abbey Farm located the exact spot of the final campsite not far from his house. All that remains of the *giant ash* is a large dip in the ground to mark where the roots of the tree once grew.

DAY FIFTEEN

Met by the Luggage Carts

Wednesday 12ᵗʰ June 1912
East Walton to Westacre (5 miles)

The arrangements for the final day had been altered. Maybe the older generation had decided that two weeks away for their daughters was really enough and Charlie Canham was needed back at Westacre for other tasks. In any event, the new arrangement was the carts from Westacre collected Judith and Win, who returned to Westacre High House with some of the luggage. Mr Howell, the footman, had come from Congham, presumably to supervise which luggage should be returned to the Elwes' home at Little Congham. Maybe Charlie Canham took Mr Howell and the Congham luggage in the Yellow Caravan and delivered it on his way past the house. Charlie Canham still had the task of returning the Yellow Caravan and the horse back to Trenny's stables at North Wootton that day, another 10 miles on for him from East Walton, but his route took him straight past Little Congham.

Got up as usual at 6 and breakfasted about 7. Poached eggs and bacon. Then began the sorting and packing. The carts were supposed to come at 9. Two came from Westacre. Judse and Win went in the pony cart and I waited to see Howell and go back in the Westacre luggage cart. While I waited I went to see the beagles with Mr Knight and alas, while absent, the luggage cart got restive and went without me! The climax! I had to walk back to Westacre from Walton! They found their loss however when the luggage cart came back without me and went to meet me but I'd nearly got to the drive gate so only 4¼ instead of 5 miles to walk. So ended our first caravan trip.

Postscript

The summer of 1912 was a wet one. We know about that from the story of the Yellow Caravan. On 13th August, the Zigamala family rented a convoy of two caravans for a family holiday—the Yellow Caravan and a green one, which they nicknamed 'The Grasshopper'. The Zigamala jaunt along the North Norfolk coast started at Heacham—convenient for Trenny as we know Heacham is where he took his family on holiday. From Hilda Zigamala's watercolours and sketches, housed in the Norfolk Archives[1], we know the Yellow Caravan had two horses to pull it all along the route, and sometimes, where it was particularly hilly, three. As they did not have Mr Canham looking after the horses at night, the horses were tethered in the camp. The Zigamala first night was rather disturbed as one of the horses used the caravan as a rubbing post, shaking up the occupants whilst they were trying to sleep. The two caravans camped at Holkham in a similar spot as Honor and Win had drawn in for the night. Later, whilst two horses were attempting to pull the Yellow Caravan up a steep sandy lane, the horses protest and try to turn downhill and almost upset the Caravan. Three horses pulled 'The Grasshopper' uphill, but on the way down it took one horse in front and seven people holding the caravan back so that it did not gather too much momentum downhill. The Zigamala party included John Zigamala, a Harrow schoolboy aged 14, and a group of his friends. They camped at Stiffkey and Sheringham, where they erected their tent on the beach so that they could change discreetly into their bathing costumes, and camped again at Cromer. They, too, suffered in the rain but appear to have got back to Rougham, Hilda Zigamala's family home, by Monday 26th August.

ഇൻൽ

The constant rain in Norfolk throughout the summer of 1912 caused the ground to become utterly waterlogged. On 26th August a great depression hovered over Norfolk, which was followed by a storm and a phenomenally heavy fall of rain when six inches fell in twelve hours and over three times the month's average rain, fell in a single day. This was accompanied by a north-westerly gale. As the land was already saturated, the water had nowhere to run to. Norwich was flooded and completely cut off. The streets were *like raging rivers*. Bridges, including Ludham Bridge, were swept away. Swaffham Rural District Council issued a directive to their surveyor in September 1912 that the roads should be

---

1 *Norfolk Record Office MC 2738/13*

repaired and to report on which places should be steam rolled in order to return them to the same condition they were in before the flood damage.

ഇഝ

Lucy Pelham Burn was politically motivated. First, as a Conservative at the age of 22, she had campaigned in the 1910 election in North Norfolk against the Liberal candidate, Noel Buxton. He was 20 years her senior when they married in 1914. He then became a Socialist in 1919 and won the North Norfolk seat for Labour in 1922, which he held until 1930 on his elevation to the Peerage, taking the title Lord Noel-Buxton. His wife Lucy then stood as the Labour candidate in the North Norfolk by-election which she won by 139 votes—but she lost her seat in 1931. She returned to the House of Commons in the Labour landslide of 1945. She died in 1960 aged 72.

ഇഝ

So many friends and acquaintances were to lose their lives during 'The Great War' of 1914-1918 and a number of them were associated with the two-week holiday adventure of the Yellow Caravan.

The Agent they met at Dunston, who looked after the girls so well when they camped there, **John Beck**, was born at Melton Constable, married Margery Kidner in April 1914 and his only son Roger was born a year later. John Beck, like his uncle Frank Beck at Sandringham, was originally in the Norfolk Regiment. From the Roll of Honour at Greshams School we learn that he received his commission in 1915 and became a Captain and Adjutant with the Kings Royal Rifle Corps. He went to the Front in August 1916 and won the Military Cross in October that year for gallant and distinguished service in the field. He was killed in action on 16th August 1917 south of Ypres and is buried in the cemetery there. His Commanding Officer wrote to his widow, *I never knew anyone so unobtrusively and persistently brave. His sympathy and care for his men was so deeply genuine that he had no time to worry about his own danger. (His death) was a bad moment for all of us, because he was loved by everyone.* John Beck is also remembered on the attractive war memorial in (the rarely open) Stoke Holy Cross church. His name is among the list of twelve on the central panel of a painted triptych with St. George and St. Michael in ornate painted panels either side.

ഇഝ

Christel Cubitt at Honing was to lose three of her five brothers. Randall and Victor Cubitt both lost their lives with the Norfolk Regiment, which was decimated at Gallipoli on 12th August 1915. This was a dreadful day for Norfolk when it was reported that 1,000 men vanished. Eustace Cubitt, having survived Gallipoli, returned to Egypt with Gervase Birkbeck and the Norfolk Yeomanry.

Eustace was killed in the third battle of Gaza in April 1917, where 200 men of the Norfolk Regiment were lost in a single day.

⊗⊃○⊗

The household at Necton was another one that was to suffer dreadfully in World War One. Not only was **Humfrey Mason** killed at Gallipoli on 12th August 1915—whose loss is recorded on a brass plaque in Necton church—on the same day as two of the Cubitt brothers but his sister Audrey also lost her husband Arthur Ward in the same action on the same day.

⊗⊃○⊗

Honor, when she arrives at East Walton, mentions that the Beauchamp family have just left Abbey Farmhouse and Mr Knight is going to move in. **Montagu Harry Proctor Beauchamp** had been a missionary in China and returned to England in 1911 to serve as a Chaplain with the British Army. During their stay in England at Abbey Farm, East Walton, his three sons, two of whom were born in China, attended a boarding school run by The Reverend Brereton and his wife at nearby Little Massingham: Montagu was 17, Ivor was 10 and Basil was 4 years old. In the First World War, Montagu joined the Norfolk Regiment and with his uncle Horace Proctor-Beauchamp from Langley, who was a Lieutenant-Colonel in the Regiment, they served together in the Dardenelles. Uncle and nephew both lost their lives at Gallipoli on 12th August 1915, when the Regiment was decimated.

⊗⊃○⊗

Gervase Birkbeck, of whom Honor was particularly fond, wrote to her from the Dardenelles and from Egypt. Her later diary of the 1914-1918 war includes Gervase's letters to her from the Dardenelles from where he was fortunate enough to return to Egypt to what was left of the Regiment. But in April 1917 Gervase was killed in Gaza aged 30, along with his friend Eustace Cubitt, when the Regiment again suffered great losses. Gervase's elder brother, Major Harry Birkbeck, also with the Norfolk Yeomanry, won the M.C. in Egypt and returned safely when the war was over to run the estate at Westacre.

⊗⊃○⊗

In the last 100 days of the war, faithful **Ted Smith**, who was photographed with Win mowing the lawn at Little Congham and who managed to drop the sack of coal on her foot at the start of the Yellow Caravan journey, was killed in France. Young **John Zigamala** lost his life at Archangel fighting for the White Russians in 1919.

⊗⊃○⊗

After a long courtship, **Una Barclay**, who was nursing during the First World War, married in 1915 Colonel Gerald T. Bullard of the Bullard brewing family, from Hellesdon House near Norwich. Gerald and Una's first home together was at Northrepps in a house rented from the Gurney family. In the autumn of 1930 Colonel Bullard bought Wood Hill at Gressenhall but sadly died of pneumonia within months of the purchase, at the age of 54. Una Bullard was an enthusiastic horsewoman who rode side-saddle all her life. Her great loves were horses and flowers and she was said to have an encyclopaedic knowledge of both. Una also loved boats and the sea. During the Second World War she worked helping to find homes for evacuated children and families for which she was awarded the B.E.M.. When times were good, Una Bullard gave wonderful parties for young people at her home. She died in 1973 at the age of 87, grandmother to many Norfolk children.

෪෧

The attentive **Dick Buxton** married in the summer of 1914 Primrose Ralli from Stanhoe—one who had signed her name in the Northrepps Visitors' Book for June 1912 during the Yeomanry Camp there. They were on their honeymoon in Scotland when World War One broke out. Petygards became the home of Dick and Prim, who later rented more acreage nearby. They continued to live at Petygards until 1944 when they purchased the striking flint and Dutch-gabled Wiveton Hall on the north Norfolk coast, which remains in their family.

෪෧

In 1914, at the outbreak of hostilities, **Charlie Canham** went back into the Marines and when the First World War was over he returned to Norfolk and set up home with his wife Ellen in an attractive street of Edwardian terraced houses in Kings Lynn. He became an Omnibus inspector and later moved to Norwich where he died aged 79 in 1960.

෪෧

In the First World War **Judith Birkbeck** became a Red Cross nurse in Rouen in Northern France and in 1917 married the Rev. Jack Thornton, who was serving in France as Chaplain to the West Yorkshire Regiment. During the late 1930s Jack Thornton became Rector of North Creake and after the Second World War Rector of East Walton. Judith died in 1966 and Jack in 1969. They are both buried in the churchyard at East Walton under the East window. Poignantly this was the same village where Judith and her cousins spent their last night with the Yellow Caravan.

෪෧

Win Elwes left home in 1914 and her first job was a scrubber at Cawston Park

Hospital. She then joined the Voluntary Aid Detachment of the Red Cross—the VAD (nicknamed the *Very Adorable Darlings*), and became an ambulance driver in Northern France. Win was awarded the M.M. for her bravery there (the highest award possible for a woman) for rescuing wounded from near a burning ammunition dump during a bombing raid. Whilst working in France, Win met a French Captain Edgar Le Coq, an interpreter for the British Army. After the First War they were married (1919) in the Roman Catholic Chapel at Oxborough. Far from wishing to tell the people of Norfolk about her distinguished achievement, Win simply brushed it aside to get on with the next task in hand. The Le Coqs travelled to Ceylon, where Edgar helped to run the Elwes family tea estates. Win returned to Norfolk in 1922 to her mother's house in Grimston for the birth of her son Jim. Later still, in order to educate Jim, Win set up and ran her own chocolate manufacturing business at Manton, Rutland. At the start of the Second World War, it is no surprise to learn that Win was back in uniform again teaching mechanics to the FANYs—the First Aid Nursing Yeomanry.

ഔൽ

Honor Elwes never married, but passed on to generations of children her enthusiasm for Norfolk. She drove a little Austin 7 and delighted in Norfolk's 'highways and byways', its churches and old buildings, nature study, wild flowers and other country-loving pursuits. During the First World War, Honor was able to keep a daily diary of events in wartime as she followed happenings on land and sea from the newspapers and letters she received from her friends and cousins at the front. She also recorded events around west Norfolk villages in wartime. Honor's diary runs into 12 handwritten

Honor in 1913 aged 23.

volumes and it is doubtful whether she ever opened any of them again so great were the losses of her friends and relations. Honor moved to the next village, Roydon, where she lived at The Old Rectory and wrote several books: *Fairy Tales from Norfolk* published 1914, *Slaminayiaf Stories* (published 1928 by Clement Ingleby) and two books of essays *Bits and Pieces* and *More Bits and Pieces*. Fifty fairy stories Honor wrote for children were never published. These included such titles as *Silverdown of the Salt Marshes*, *The Cry of the Redshank* and *When the Moon was Young* all of which exist in manuscript in her firm, clear hand. Honor died in 1959 and both she and her sister Win are remembered in the churchyard at Congham.

Appendix I

Some Recipes From 1912

Mrs Beeton's Cookery Book was first published as a book in 1861 and was an immediate best-seller, with 60,000 copies in its first year. By 1868 sales were totalling nearly two million. In 1912 recipes were also available in magazines. Although they lived in houses with staff, all three young ladies would have had supervised cooking lessons in the kitchen at their homes. Win and Honor from Miss Ellen Parish at Congham and Judith from Miss Annie Price in the kitchen at Westacre.

Green Pea Soup (using fresh peas)

Required: One pint of green peas, three pints of thin stock, two ounces of bacon, one onion, a bay leaf, sweet herbs, a few spinach leaves. Boil all the ingredients together and, when quite tender, pass the peas and spinach leaves through a sieve, adding as much of the liquor as is required to make it of the consistency of thin cream. Return to the saucepan, heat it, adding a teaspoonful of caster sugar, and pepper and salt to taste. Serve with small dice of fried bread.

Green Pea Soup (using dried peas)

Required: ½ lb dried peas, 1 onion, carrot, turnip, a stick of celery, 3 pints stock, a small handful of mint. Salt & pepper, ½ oz flour, ½ teaspoon bicarbonate of soda. Wash the peas, cover with boiling water and add the bicarbonate of soda. Leave to soak overnight. Drain and rinse in cold water. Peel and slice the vegetables and place with the peas, stock and mint in a saucepan. Season with salt and pepper and bring to the boil and simmer for about two hours. Rub through a sieve, removing the mint first. Blend the flour with a little water and add to the soup while re-heating. Stir continuously and simmer for five minutes before serving.

Spring Soup

Ingredients: Two quarts of clear beef stock, three turnips, two carrots, two

133

onions, celery, two lettuces, sorrel, half a pint of asparagus tops, salt, pepper. *Method*: Pare the turnips and carrots and cut them into marbles or small dice, cut the white stem part of the celery into small pieces and the onions in rings, then in fine shreds; boil up the stock, put in the prepared vegetables and let it simmer for forty minutes, adding salt and pepper; wash, dry and tear the lettuces up, put them and the sorrel leaves into the soup and boil until all the vegetables are tender; boil the asparagus tops separately just before taking up the soup, put them in, boil for a minute or two, then serve.

Shrimp Toast

Ingredients: ¼ pint peeled shrimps, anchovy paste, ½ oz butter, 1 egg, 1 tablespoonful milk, cayenne, 8 croutes of buttered toast. *Method:* Melt the butter in a stew-pan, put in the shrimps and when hot add the eggs and milk previously beaten together, salt and cayenne to taste, stir by the fire until the mixture thickens. Meanwhile spread the croûtes of buttered toast lightly with anchovy paste and then add shrimp preparation and serve hot.

Baked Mackerel

Take care that the fish are very fresh. This will be known by the brilliancy of the skin and the stiffness of the body. Wash and dry two mackerel, remove the gut, cut off the heads and tails, split them down the back and take out the bones. Grease a baking-tin with butter, place one mackerel on it, skin downwards, sprinkle over it two table-spoonful's of breadcrumbs mixed with two tea-spoonful's of chopped parsley or fennel, a quarter of a teaspoonful of mixed herbs, one finely-chopped shallot, one ounce of butter cut into small pieces, half a teaspoonful of salt, and a good sprinkling of pepper; place the other fish on the top, skin upwards, put small bits of butter on it; bake for nearly a quarter of an hour, basting frequently.

Eel Pie

Ingredients: One pound of eels, a little chopped parsley, one shallot, grated nutmeg, pepper and salt, the juice of half a lemon, forcemeat, stock, puff-paste (pastry). Method: Skin and wash the eels, cut them into pieces two inches long and line the bottom of the pie dish with forcemeat. Put in the eels and sprinkle them with parsley, shallot, nutmeg, seasoning and lemon juice. Pour in the stock, cover with puff-paste; bake for one hour or rather more.

Poached Trout

Clean, de-scale and gut the fish. Place in fish kettle, or large pan and cover with cold water. Add a couple of bay leaves and bring slowly to the boil. Allow to bubble once or twice, then remove pan from heat, cover and allow to cool. Serve warm or cold.

Fried Rabbit

Ingredients: One or two rabbits, egg, breadcrumbs, salt, pepper, butter or lard. Method: Wash and soak the rabbit well, put it into boiling water and let it boil for six or seven minutes; drain it well and let it get cold. Cut it up in joints, dip them into beaten egg, then into breadcrumbs, and fry in boiling butter or lard over a moderate fire from twelve to fifteen minutes. Boil the liver of the rabbit, let it cool and mince it up; put a little gravy or stock into a pan, put in the liver, thicken the gravy with flour and butter, season with salt, pepper and lemon-juice. Dish up the rabbit, pour the gravy round, garnish with small three corner pieces of toast and serve.

Compote of Pigeon

Ingredients: Three pigeons, half a pound of streaky bacon, butter, flour, a pint of stock, a few small onions. Method: Cut the bacon in small pieces and fry it gently in a stew-pan with a small bit of butter; when slightly browned take it out and put in the pigeons trussed for boiling. When they have fried for a short time and are browned, lift them out, stir a large tablespoon of flour into the fat and when this is brown add the boiling stock very slowly, stirring it all the time. Put back the birds, bacon and onions and stew very gently for three quarters of an hour. Dish up the pigeons on the bacon, put the onions round, skim the gravy, pour it round the birds and serve.

To boil a Fowl

Clean and truss for boiling. Fill cavity with onions and skewer firmly. Cover with greased paper and tie firmly. Put in boiling water with 1 onion, 1 carrot, 1 turnip, bunch of parsley, pepper and salt. Simmer gently. Chicken ½ hour, fowl 1–2 hours, depending on age. Remove from pan. Remove paper, string and skewers. Serve hot or cold.

Chaudfroid of Chicken

Boil a young fowl in nicely-flavoured stock, or, if you have not the latter, add carrot, onion, turnips and a bouquet garni to the water. When cold take the skin off the fowl, cut into neat joints, dissolve an ounce and a half of fresh butter in a small saucepan, stir into it an ounce of flour, and when quite smooth gradually add half a pint of well-flavoured white sauce and two sheets of leaf gelatine, previously soaked in the cold stock; bring to the boil, add sufficient cream to whiten the sauce, and squeeze of lemon-juice. Mask each joint of chicken with the sauce, decorate with truffle or yolk of egg. When the sauce is quite set make a nice salad, mixed with mayonnaise sauce, in the centre of a dish, pile the chicken round, and garnish with cucumber slices, radishes or any other garnish preferred.

Mock Turtle

Mock Turtle is a most useful dish where a substantial one is wanted.

Required: One small shoulder of mutton, one dozen tinned oysters, breadcrumbs, half a teaspoonful of ground mace and the same of pepper, one onion stuck with cloves, four long pepper, one ounce of butter, one ounce of flour.

Take the shoulder of mutton, bone it, and lay it skin side downwards on a chopping board, sprinkle with the pepper and mace, lay on it the oysters, cover with breadcrumbs, and season with pepper and salt. Roll the meat neatly, sew down the flap, and tie round with tape. Place the meat in a saucepan with a small quantity of water, the onion, cloves and long pepper. Cover closely and turn once while cooking. Twenty minutes should be allowed for every pound of meat, and it should cook very slowly. Take a pint of stock, thicken with an ounce of flour, work into it an ounce of butter. Flavour the sauce nicely, and add a teaspoonful of chopped gherkins. Place the meat on a hot dish, remove the tape, and pour the sauce over. Garnish the meat with slices of gherkin, and serve.

Devilled Sardines

Ingredients: 6 sardines, 1 oz. butter, 1 teaspoon flour, salt, cayenne, 1 teaspoon dry mustard, fried bread, 1 teaspoon grated Parmesan cheese. *Method:* Skin and bone the sardines. Divide them into fillets. Spread the fillets with the mixture of butter, mustard, flour, cheese, salt and cayenne well mixed. Then toss the fillets up in a little butter and serve on fingers of fried bread.

Onion and Kidney Dumplings

Ingredients: 8 oz. self-raising flour, ½ teaspoon salt, 4 oz. margarine or 2 oz margarine and 2 oz. Cooking fat. Cold water for mix. Filling: 4 medium Spanish onions ¼ lb. ox kidney or 2 sheep's kidneys, salt and pepper, beaten eggs. *Method:* Peel the onions, put them into cold water and bring to the boil. Strain off the water, cover again with cold water and cook until tender and unbroken. Allow to cool. Meanwhile cut the kidney into small pieces, season and just cover with cold water and cook until tender. Remove the centre carefully from the onions. Chop them, add the kidney and seasoning and mix well. Prepare the pastry. Cut into four and roll each piece into a round. Brush the edges of the rounds with beaten egg or water. Put one onion on each round and fill the centres with kidney. Meantime, bring the edges of pasty together, press well and turn the dumplings over. Brush with beaten egg. Place on a greased baking sheet and bake in fairly hot oven for 20 minutes.

Brown Sauce

Ingredients: 1 oz. self-raising flour, ½ pt. stock or water, 1 small onion, small piece of carrot, a little celery (if available) salt and pepper. *Method*: Melt the dripping, fry the chopped onion, carrot and celery until brown. Lift out and drain well. Add the flour and fry until brown stirring all the time. Add a little bone dripping if required. Stir in the liquid gradually and bring to the boil; add seasoning and vegetables. Simmer for ½ hour stirring frequently. Strain and use as required.

Saute New Potatoes

Ingredients: One pound and a half of potatoes, three ounces of butter, pepper and salt. Choose small potatoes for this, and let them be of as even size as possible. *Method*: Rub them clean, and dry perfectly. Melt the butter in a saucepan, and put in the potatoes. Keep tossing them over the fire till they are of a uniform golden colour. Add white pepper and salt to taste, and serve.

To Boil Sea Kale

Cut off any part that may be at all green, lay in cold water and wash it clean. Put into boiling water with salt and boil quickly for 20 minutes. Have a slice of toasted bread in the dish. Take out the kale with a fish slice and dish up on the toast, laying it all one way, and pour butter sauce over.

Baked Onions

Ingredients: Spanish onions, minced meat, salt, pepper, butter. Method: Peel the onions, remove a little of the centre, fill up the hole with well-seasoned minced meat, put the onions into an earthenware pot, with a little butter and water or stock. Bake them in a good oven for about two hours, or until they are quite tender; add more stock if they should get too dry; dish them up, pour the stock round, and serve.

Stock recipe

Required: For three quarts of stock: 4 lbs bones, 2 carrots, 2 onions, a few cloves, a bunch of herbs, pepper and salt. Average cost: 9d. Chop the bones and put them with the vegetables, seasoning and herbs into an airtight vessel and boil for eight hours. Then strain and when cold remove the fat. This forms a useful and cheap stock for soups and sauces.

Norfolk Dumplings

1 oz. baking powder, 1 lb. flour, a little salt. Make into a dough and cut off into ¼ lb. weight dumplings. Let it rise a little while then boil for 20 minutes being careful not to let them stick to the bottom of the pan.

Cornflour Pudding

(From the 1910 Advertisement for Brown & Polson's 'Patent' Corn Flour)

You know how delicious and how good blancmange with stewed fruit is. Have the blancmange perfect in this way:

Use only good sweet milk (1½ pints to 2 oz. of Brown & Polson's 'Patent' Corn Flour). Blend the Corn Flour with a little of the milk, while bringing the rest to the boil. Add the blended Corn Flour slowly. Then while stirring boil the whole for ten minutes. This makes such a delicious blancmange with a flavour entirely different from one not properly made.

Blancmange—tip

If the white of an egg well beaten up is added to each pint of cornflour or ground rice blancmange before the mixture is poured into moulds, the blancmange will be softer and lighter.

Stewed Gooseberries

Stewed gooseberries are only too often sent to the table in a pulpy mass: however if properly cooked each berry will remain whole. The best way to attain this result is to put the fruit in a jar with a little hot water and enough sugar to sweeten it, cover the top of the jar with paper, a cloth, or a lid, and stand it in a saucepan of boiling water. Let the water boil for one hour, and by that time you will find that the gooseberries are thoroughly stewed without being in a pulp.

Gooseberry Fool

Ingredients: 1 quart of gooseberries, ¾ lb moist sugar, ½ pint water, 1 pt milk or cream. *Method:* Take the tops and tails from gooseberries and boil them with sugar and water until soft. Rub them through a hair sieve. Pour in the milk or cream gradually and serve on a glass dish.

Prune Jelly

Ingredients: One pound of large prunes, sugar, lemon, cloves, cinnamon, wine jelly, cream. *Method:* Soak the prunes in warm water all night then put them and the water into a stew pan with the spices, sugar, lemon-peel and juice and stew very gently until they are very tender but unbroken. Drain the prunes from the syrup. If possible, without spoiling the appearances of the fruit, take out the stones. Arrange a layer of the prunes in a wetted mould and pour in just enough liquid wine jelly to cover them. When the layer is firm, fill the mould with the prunes, arranging them round the sides, then fill the mould with the jelly. Let it stand in a cold place until set; turn out and garnish with whipped cream.

Light Currant Dumplings

For each dumpling take three table-spoons of flour, 2 tablespoons of finely minced suet, 3 table-spoons currants, a slight pinch of salt and as much milk or water as will make a very thick batter. Tie the dumplings in well flavoured cloths and boil them for a full hour. These are nice served with sweet sauce.

Apple Dumplings

Peel six medium sized apples very thinly and core them, but do not cut them up. Cut half a pound of short pastry into six pieces and roll each piece into a ball. Take an apple and work it into the centre of each ball of paste and put a clove and some sugar into the centre of each apple before closing the paste. Place on a greased tin and bake slowly for half an hour.

Junket

Ingredients: 1 pint of new milk, 1 gill of cream, castor sugar to taste. Rennet powder or tablets according to directions, nutmeg. *Method:* Warm the milk until it feels comfortably warm but not hot. Dissolve the rennet powder. Add the rennet to the milk, sweeten to taste. Pour at once into a Junket dish. Leave in a cool place until needed. At the last, heap whipped and sweetened cream over the top and grate over lightly with nutmeg.

Strawberry Jam Pudding

Ingredients: One teacupful of strawberry jam, one teaspoon of baking powder, one ounce of candied peel, one teacupful of flour, one teacupful of milk, two ounces of suet, one pinch of salt, jam sauce. Method: Mix the baking powder with the flour, add the salt and the suet finely minced. Mix well together, then add the jam and the candied peel; pour in the milk slowly, mixing well all the time. Butter a mould, put in the pudding and steam for two hours and a half. Serve with jam sauce of strawberry jam.

Lemonade

Required: One large lemon, two ounces of sugar, one pint of boiling water.

Method: Wipe the lemon with a damp cloth, pare the yellow rind thinly and put into a jug, pare off the white pith, and cut the fruit into thin slices removing all pith and pips; put the lemon slices into the jug, pour over the water, cover and let stand till cold. Strain and serve.

Appendix II

Wildflowers

Wild Flowers found on Chalky soil:

Sainfoin, Yellow Wort, Pyramid Orchid, Bee Orchid, Scabious, Greater Wild Thyme, Rock Rose, Hare Bell, Purple Milk Vetch, Dropwort, Lesser Birds Foot Trefoil, Bulbous Buttercup, Carline Thistle, Common Gromwell, Common Milkwort, Field Madder, and Vervain. (A number of these plants can be found growing in the chalk on the Norfolk Wildlife Trust Reserve at nearby Ringstead)

Common Wild Flowers of Marsh & Broadland:

Marsh Marigold, Ladies Smock, Ragged Robin, Water Crowfoot, Yellow Flag, Meadow Sweet, Woundwort, Water Mint, Reed, Bull Rush

Appendix III

Camping Sites Along The Route Of The Yellow Caravan welcoming visitors today

Sandringham—Country Park

Burnham—Deepdale Farm

Holkham—Pinewoods

Wells—Pinewoods on Beach Road and Blue Skies on Stiffkey Road

Stiffkey—High Sand Creek

Morston—Scaldbeck Cottage and camping

Blakeney—Galley Hill Farm, Friary Farm

Wiveton—Ambers Bell Tents

Kelling—Kelling Heath Holiday Park (Blue Sky Leisure Co.)

Weybourne—Foxhills Camping, Breck Farm

Sheringham—Woodlands *and* Mill Cottage, Upper Sheringham

Beeston—Beeston Regis Holiday Park *and* Bumble Barn Bell Tents

West Runton—West Runton Camping *and* Incleboro Fields

East Runton—Wood Hill

Cromer—The Grove Glamping *and* Cromer Camping

Overstrand—Ivy Farm

Northrepps—Forest Park *and* Shrublands Farm

Honing—Honing Hideaway

Dilham—Canal Camping

Horning—Ambers Bell Tents, Bewilderwood Hoveton

Surlingham—Alderfen Marshes

Hingham—Rectory Farm

Shipdham—Spring Farm

Necton—Clay Pit Farm

Petygards—Petygards Hall Camping

Narborough—Narborough Fisheries

East Walton—Abbey Farm

If planning a 4-night 5-day drive-round trip along the route of The Yellow Caravan, choose any combination of good hotels listed here:

Kings Lynn—Knights Hill Hotel, South Wootton

Dersingham—Rose & Crown

Burnham Market—The Hoste

Holkham—The Victoria & The Ancient House

Blakeney—Manor Hotel or Blakeney Hotel (ask for an Estuary View)

Kelling—The Pheasant

Cromer—The Grove or Hotel de Paris

Northrepps—Northrepps Cottage Country Hotel

Horning—The Swan Inn, Innkeepers Lodge Group (ask for a River View)

Dunston—Dunston Hall Hotel

Hingham—The White Hart

Swaffham—Strattons

Appendix IV

Public Houses Visited By The Yellow Caravan

The Brick Kilns, Little Plumstead

The Railway Tavern, Framingham Earl

The Red Lion (now The Wildebeest) Stoke Holy Cross

The Golden Dog, Shipdham

Sources & Further Reading

Anderson, V., *The Northrepps Grandchildren*, 1983 (Mallard)

Barnes, P., *Norfolk Landowners since 1880*, 1993 (University of East Anglia Centre of East Anglian Studies)

Bastin, J., *Norfolk Yeomanry in Peace and War*, 1986 (Iceni Press)

Birkbeck, H., *The Birkbecks of Norfolk*, 1993 (Michael Russell (Publishing) Ltd)

Butcher, B.D., *A Movable Rambling Police: A Movable Rambling Police: History of Policing in Norfolk*, 1989 (Norfolk Constabulary)

Clarke, D., *The Country Houses of Norfolk Part II Lost Houses*, 2008 (Geo R Reeve Ltd)

Cushing, G. & Starsmore I., *Steam at Thursford*, 1982 (David & Charles)

Dale, I. & Smith, J., *Honourable Ladies Volume I: Profiles of Women MPs 1918-1996*, 2018 (Biteback Publishing)

Dalton, N, & Ebdon, P. (eds), *A Wall of Water*, 1985 (Masque Community Theatre for Norfolk)

Dutt. W., *Highways and Byways of East Anglia*, 1904, (Macmillian)

Ellis, E.A., *Wild Flowers of the Waterways & Marshes*, 1972 (Jarrold Colour Publications)

Poringland Archive Group, *Poringland, Album of Past Years*

Francis, S., *Clarky Bottoms & Small Hopes, An Atlas of Place-names in the Burnhams*, Norfolk, 2009, (Sally Francis)

Gilmour, J., *Wild Flowers of the Chalk*, 1947 (Penguin)

Grahame, K., *The Wind in the Willows*, 1908, (Methuen)

Norfolk Federation of Women's Institutes, *The Norfolk Village Book*, 1999 (Countryside Books)

Stilgoe, L. & Shreeve, D., *The Round Tower Churches of Norfolk*, 2001, (Canterbury Press)

Hooton, J., *The Glaven Ports : A Maritime History of Blakeney, Cley and Wiveton in North Norfolk*, 1997 (Blakeney History Group)

Joice, D., *Full Circle*, 1991 (The Boydell Press)

Kelly, G., *The Ferry House, Surlingham*

Kenworthy- Browne, J., Sayer, M. et al., *Burke's and Savills Guide to Country Houses Volume III East Anglia*, 1981 (Burke's Peerage)

Mason, H. J., *Flint: the Versatile Stone*, 1978 (Providence Press)

McGoun, B., *A Slice of Horning Life*, 1997 (B.McGoun)

North, D. & Hayward, M., *Elements of the North Norfolk Coast: Wildlife, Villages, History, Myths Legends*, 2004 (Birdseyeview Books)

Rice, M., *Building Norfolk*, 2009 (Frances Lincoln)

Rye, J., *A Popular Guide to Norfolk Place Names*, 1991 (The Larks Press)

Skipper, K., *The Norfolk Companion*, 1994 (Jim Baldwin)

Greaves, R., *Hunting in Norfolk and Suffolk*, 1951 (Field Sports Publications)

Spencer, N., *Sculptured Monuments in Norfolk Churches*, 1997 (Norfolk Churches Trust)

Steers, J.A., *Blakeney Point and Scolt Head Island, Norfolk*, 1964 (The National Trust)

The Burnham Society History Group, *The Book of the Burnhams: The Story of the Seven Burnhams by the Sea*, 2011

Wade-Martins, P. (ed), *Historical Atlas of Norfolk*, 1993 (Norfolk Museums Service)

Wilton, J.W., *Monastic Life in Norfolk and Suffolk*, 1980 (Acorn Editions)

Index

You may also like:

Norfolk Documents 1

Mr Marten's Travels in East Anglia

The 1825 Journal of Robert Humphrey Marten

EDITED BY Elizabeth Larby

available from local bookshops and
www.poppyland.co.uk